MOTHERLAND

West Indian Women to Britain
in the 1950s

Elyse Dodgson

Sylvia L. Collicott

Heinemann Educational Books Ltd
22 Bedford Square, London WC1B 3HH
LONDON EDINBURGH MELBOURNE AUCKLAND
HONG KONG SINGAPORE KUALA LUMPUR NEW DELHI
IBADAN NAIROBI JOHANNESBURG
PORTSMOUTH (NH) KINGSTON PORT OF SPAIN

© Elyse Dodgson 1984
First published 1984

ISBN 0 435 23230 4

All rights whatsoever in this play are reserved and on no account may performances be given unless written permission has been obtained before rehearsals commence from the Motherland Company c/o 3 Aubert Road, London N5.

Line drawings by Mary Hackbarth
Drawing at foot of p. 47 by Pete Jones
Photographs from the BBC Hulton Picture Library
Photograph on p. 67 by Sinclair Ashman

Printed in Great Britain by
Thomson Litho Ltd, East Kilbride, Scotland

CONTENTS

Acknowledgements	iv

Part One: Background Notes, Testimony, Developments

Introduction		2
1	Reasons for Leaving	5
2	Preparing and Parting	13
3	First Impressions	19
4	Housing	25
5	Earning a Living	31
6	Childcare	37
7	Relationships with Men	43
8	Responses to the 'New Community'	49
9	Bringing up Children	55
10	On Women	61

Part Two: The Play *Motherland*

Introduction	68
Motherland	71

Part Three: The Drama Lessons

Introduction		98
The Lessons:		
1	Reasons for Leaving	100
2	Preparing and Parting	102
3	First Impressions	104
4	Housing	106
5	Earning a Living	108
6	Childcare	110
7	Relationships with Men	112
8	Responses to the 'New Community'	114
9	Bringing up Children	116
10	On Women	118

Suggested Reading	120
Bibliography	122

In memory of Vauxhall Manor Girls' School
'Hay una mujer desaparecida...'

Acknowledgements

This book has depended upon the support of a great many people. It is not possible to name them all, but I should like to give my special thanks to:

the women who were interviewed:
Dolly Adams, Hepsibah Archer, Maude Banton, Clarissa Booth, Ruby Brown, Constance Gayle, Dawn Hinds, Vera James, Gwen Johnson, Betty King, Monica Masters, Bertha McLean, Cherryl Monteith, Marion Morris, Velma Moseley, Hilda Riley, Betty Russell, Edna Saunders, Marlene Shorey, Dorothy Smith, Stephanie Swinton, Mona Williamson;

Marcia Smith who conducted the interviews and helped to co-ordinate the Motherland Project;

the Motherland Company;

the staff of Vauxhall Manor School, 1978—83, particularly:
Terri Carey, Rob Cox, Denise Gilbert, Ros Gillham, Mary Hackbarth, Cathy Herman, Pete Jones, Dilly McDermott, Chris Parker, Les Scarfe, Alison Seal, Joan Smith, Europe Singh, Sid Willis, Jane Woodall, Adrienne Wratten;

the Oval House Staff Team;

and the following groups and individuals:
ACER Project, Carol Adams, Ambit Editorial Group, Black Pensioners Club at Stockwell Good Neighbours, Donald Hinds, Hulton Picture Library, ILEA Division 9 Inspectorate, ILEA Drama Inspectorate, Institute of Race Relations Library, London Drama, and Jon Nixon who discussed this book with me throughout its making.

Part One
BACKGROUND NOTES, TESTIMONY, DEVELOPMENTS

Introduction

The accounts you are about to read are taken from interviews with twenty-three West Indian women who live in the community surrounding Vauxhall Manor School in south London*. They were all interviewed as part of a project which focussed on the migration of West Indian women to Britain in the 1950s. These interviews were used as a basis for the play *Motherland* (see Part Two) and the classroom work in Part Three.

This type of project is sometimes referred to as *oral history*; that is, it was concerned with finding out about the past by listening to the voices of the people who took part in it. It is through this questioning of people about their past that we can put on record not only what people did, but what they felt about it as well. Through the project pupils were able to make valuable links between their own experience and that of the women who were interviewed.

It is important to note that when we refer to the West Indies we are talking about islands which cover a very wide area. There are, for example, over 1,000 miles between Jamaica, the largest island in the north-west, and Trinidad in the extreme south-east which faces the coast of South America. The islands that the women came from were British colonies and all had a particular social and economic relationship to Britain (see map on p. 9). However, each island had its own history and traditions.

The twenty-three women came from different islands for different reasons and at different stages in their lives. Cherryl Monteith came from Jamaica when she was eleven to join her parents in 1957; Dolly Adams came from Trinidad in 1955 with her young daughter to join her husband; Marlene Shorey came from Barbados in 1960 for better working opportunities. All the accounts are taken from what the women actually said. None of the women, however, claims to speak for all West Indian women. Each of the voices is unique. The women speak for themselves and themselves alone.

---

*This school no longer exists. It amalgamated with a local boys' school to become Lilian Baylis School in September, 1983.

The first part of the book is divided into ten sections, each covering a theme that was explored in depth throughout the project. Each section is introduced by background notes which give more detailed information about the social history of the period. Some primary sources are also included: photographs taken from the British magazine *Picture Post* which was a popular weekly in the 1950s, and advertisements taken from the *Daily Gleaner* published in Kingston, Jamaica, at the height of the migration in 1955. The illustrated testimony is then followed by suggestions for developing the work further. All the developments involve you in gathering a certain amount of information and becoming aware of issues relevant to that particular section. It is important to think about why you are performing a particular task or engaging in a particular activity. The aim ultimately is to increase your own understanding of certain themes relating to the migration of West Indian women to Britain in the 1950s.

Note on Terminology

I am aware of the controversy over the use of the term 'West Indian' and the belief that the term has colonial overtones which the term 'Caribbean' does not carry. However, the former term is used throughout this book primarily because it was used by the women who were interviewed to describe their own cultural identity and origins and, secondly, because it is the standard term in the documents, historical literature, poetry and fiction of the time.

DAILY GLEANER, WEDNESDAY, OCTOBER 5, 1955.

BOOK NOW
AND TRAVEL IN COMFORT TO
ENGLAND

If you're planning to go to England let us plan it for you. No matter how you want to travel we can take all the worry and trouble out of your trip for you.

By Plane — Sept. & Oct.	£85.
By Boat — Sept. 10th. & 12th Oct. 3rd., 16th & 25th	£75.
By Plane & Boat — Sept. 11th	£87.14

COXE BROS
TRAVEL AGENTS

Opportunity Direct To
PLYMOUTH by Ship
OCT. 14 & 28
£75
To London
Oct. 16 — £75

CARIBBEAN TOURS (Ja.)
21 Church St.
Phones 5579 — 43325

SHIPPING AND AIR SERVICE

EMBARKATION NOTICE

THE M.S.
"ANDREA GRITTI"
will sail from KINGSTON
THURSDAY, OCT. 6th.

Baggage not required during the voyage MUST BE DELIVERED to the Baggage Master at **NO. 1 PIER** between the hours of **8.00 a.m. & 3.00 p.m.** TODAY — WEDNESDAY 5th.

Embarkation will commence at 8 a.m. Thursday, Oct. 6th, and ship will depart in the afternoon. Lunch will be served on board to passengers embarked.

Contact Your
TRAVEL AGENT
For Your TICKETS
IMMEDIATELY!

- M/V FRANCESCO MOROSINI .... SEPT. 15
- S/S AURIGA .... SEPT. 12
- M/V SANTA MARIA ...... OCT. 3
- M/V ANDREA GRITTI .... OCT. 6
- S/S NASSAU .... OCT. 28

GO DIRECT to Plymouth
ENGLAND
aboard the POPULAR and DEPENDABLE
S.S. "AURIGA"

THE FINEST TRAVEL VALUE
available for your voyage to ENGLAND!

BOOK NOW
and be sure of your reservations...
SEE YOUR TRAVEL AGENT TODAY
and say
"AURIGA"

SAILING FOR PLYMOUTH ON
Oct. 28th
ACCOMMODATIONS NOW AVAILABLE at
£75

Fratelli-Grimaldi Shipping Line
General Agents:
Lascelles, deMercado & Co., Ltd.

WARNING!

No foodstuffs or fruits must be packed in your baggage. Arrangements have been made for your baggage to arrive in London at the same time as the passenger. All your baggage must be small packages to enable them to go on the same train after you have disembarked from the boat.

Philip Seaga
TRAVEL ADVISERS LTD.
43 ORANGE ST. — KINGSTON
PASSENGER AGENTS FOR THE SIDARMA LINE

IF YOU'RE BURDENED WITH PACKETS
IF YOU HAVE A WEE KIT
YOU'LL SAVE ON YOUR TICKET
IF YOU BUY IT THRU' KITS

TO ENGLAND ONLY £75

FOR TRAVEL ANYWHERE AND EVERYWHERE
BY SEA AND AIR,
CONTACT:
KINGSTON INTERNATIONAL TRAVEL SERVICE LTD.
60 EAST ST., KINGSTON   TELEPHONE 34961

1 Reasons for Leaving

BACKGROUND NOTES

West Indian migration

The West Indian migration to Britain in the 1950s was part of a history of migration from the Caribbean Islands which had started over one hundred years before. It began with the migration of former slaves, very soon after emancipation in 1834. As free men and women many soon discovered that there was little opportunity and hardly any fertile land left for them to develop. One of the means of overcoming their poverty was to leave their island altogether — to migrate. Migration was also thought to be a form of protest whereby former slaves could demonstrate their hatred of a system that had tied them for so long to one place.

Since the abolition of slavery, succeeding generations of West Indians have travelled to other countries in search of work: to build the Panama Canal (between the years 1881 and 1911) and to the United States where they were recruited for agricultural work (before immigration controls in 1924 and during the Second World War). In the 1920s Jamaican women migrated in large numbers to Cuba where there were jobs in laundry, dressmaking and domestic work. Many migrants also travelled to work the coffee and banana plantations in Honduras and Costa Rica and the oil refineries in Venezuela. During the Second World War thousands of West Indians joined the British and, later, American armed forces and war industries. Others joined as 'Overseas Volunteer Workers' in Britain.

Migration to Britain

The growth of the British economy has at times been dependent upon the movement of a large number of workers from farms to the towns, from the towns to the colonies and, more recently, from the ex-colonies and poorer parts of Europe to the industrial centres of Britain. In the nineteenth century the building of the canals and railways alone caused the arrival of over 700,000 Irish immigrants. Refugee Jews and Ukrainians in the 1880s provided a valuable supplement to the labour force.

At times this flow of labour has been deliberately encouraged and at others it has been subject to political controls. For example, the 1905 Aliens Act became the first major restriction on immigration. This was due to a wave of hostility directed against Ukrainians, Jews and others who had entered the country.

The first phase of black migration into Britain took place during the time of Elizabeth I (although there is evidence of black men and women in Britain in pre-Roman times). This occurred with the introduction of slaves to serve the aristocracy, but not all Africans were enslaved domestics. Some had gained their freedom, some had always been independent, while a few possessed property. (For more information about early black settlement in Britain see Suggested Reading.)

After the Second World War the economic boom in Britain and the number of workers killed meant that it was advantageous to recruit labour from overseas. Initially prisoners of war and refugees in Europe were recruited for various workers' schemes.

West Indian migration to Britain after the Second World War

Many studies of West Indian emigration to Britain have described a variety of 'push' factors which caused West Indians to leave their islands and 'pull' factors which attracted them to England. This 'push' and 'pull' model may prove a helpful way of examining some of the reasons for leaving.

Push factors, which caused West Indians to leave their islands, basically stem from the underdeveloped state of the economy which is attributed to the islands' colonial relationship with Britain. In other words, Britain benefited by obtaining cheap raw materials from her colonies while at the same time the colonies provided a market for the finished products produced in the 'mother country'. In the West Indies as a whole, immediately following the Second World War, there was a further deterioration of economic conditions. There was overpopulation, large-scale unemployment, low wage-levels and a lack of adequate opportunities for education and vocational training.

The major *pull factors* which attracted West Indians to England are derived from the economic boom in post-war Britain which left many job vacancies. For West Indian migrants there was then the promise of year-round jobs, higher wages, and better opportunities for education and vocational training. However significant these 'push' and 'pull' factors may be, it is important to stress that they will never be felt equally by everyone in the population. Some people will decide to migrate, while others will decide to remain where they are. Still others will not be able to afford the fare.

McCarren Walter Act, 1952

An important factor which boosted West Indian migration to Britain was the passing of the McCarren Walter Act by the United States Congress in 1952. This limited the number of British West Indians who could enter the USA from 65,000 to just 800 a year. Prior to this Act the USA was a preferred place of settlement by many West Indians. It was nearer; it was richer; it already had a large established West Indian community.

The passing of this legislation, which aimed to limit the number of immigrants to the USA and determine the nationality of those who would be let in, caused much resentment throughout the Caribbean. Having been deprived of the American outlet, West Indians were forced to explore other avenues for migration. Britain, with its 'open door' policy which gave all Commonwealth citizens the status of British citizens, seemed a natural choice.

Britain as the 'mother country'

Most of the women who were interviewed for this project spoke of how Britain was portrayed in the West Indies as the 'mother country'. As children they had celebrated the same national holidays and the coronation of King George VI and Queen Elizabeth II. They had also celebrated Empire Day which was described to them as 'a demonstration for the solidarity of Britain and her colonies'. Some felt that there was more emphasis on loyalty to England at school than to your own island. As one of the interviewees stated: 'There was patriotism and a feeling that you would belong. It really was the mother country and being away from home wouldn't be that terrible because you would belong.'

Recruitment campaigns

Before mass emigration to Britain got underway, people had to learn about available opportunities. As thousands of West Indians came to Britain during the war, ex-servicemen who remained in Britain wrote home about job opportunities. Once the emigration began in the early 1950s, reports from friends and relatives also became an important source of information. As the number of travel agencies in the West Indies increased, advertisements began to appear in the local newspapers (see those from the Jamaican *Daily Gleaner*, p. 4).

The economic expansion in post-war Britain provided better pay and higher-status jobs for the workers there, creating openings on the lower rung of the occupational ladder. Therefore recruitment from overseas and the ex-colonies appeared to be an attractive proposition. Both government and industry set up job centres throughout the West Indies and started claiming that 'the welfare state' offered full employment for all. Agents were employed to organize recruitment drives. The National Health Service established job centres in order to attract nursing staff to British hospitals. In Barbados state-aided systems of emigration got underway; London Transport recruited bus crews; and the British Hotels and Restaurants' Association recruited workers for their industry.

Migration of women

In the early years of post-war migration a higher proportion of men left for England than women. According to Nancy Foner in her study of Jamaican migrants in London: 'Men seemed to receive preference as the expected family providers in amassing funds to pay for the passage' (Foner, 1981, p. 12).

By the mid-1950s through the early 1960s, the proportion of women entering Britain rose. In 1951, some 15,000 persons born in the West Indies were resident in the UK. Of the total, 37 per cent were women. The 1961 census return showed a total of 172,379 British West Indian born people residing in the UK. Of these 96,070 were male and 76,309 were female. (Most experts believe these figures to be a rather low estimate — see Table 1 below.)

Although many women came to England to join a spouse or relative, it is difficult to generalize about women's reasons for leaving. Many also came in response to employment opportunities. Some migrated alone and prior to their spouses. Women, like men, have had a history of responding to employment opportunities abroad.

Table 1 (from Peach, 1968, p. 15)

The statistics below were compiled by the Migrant Services Division of the West Indian Federation Office and place the total number of West Indians entering the United Kingdom as 238,000 persons by 1961.

Emigrants as Percentage of West Indian Populations

	Population from 1960 census*	Total emigration to UK 1955–61†	Emigrants as percentage of population
Jamaica	1,609,814	148,369	9.2
Barbados	232,085	18,741	8.1
Trinidad and Tobago	825,700	9,610	1.2
British Guiana	558,769	7,141	1.3
Leewards	122,920	16,025	13.0
Antigua	54,060	4,687	8.7
Montserrat	12,167	3,835	31.5
St Kitts-Nevis-Anguilla	56,693	7,503	13.2
Windwards	314,995	27,154	8.6
Dominica	59,479	7,915	13.3
Grenada	88,617	7,663	8.6
St Lucia	86,194	7,291	8.5
St Vincent	80,705	4,285	5.3

*Provisional figures. †Jamaica 1953–61, M.S.D.

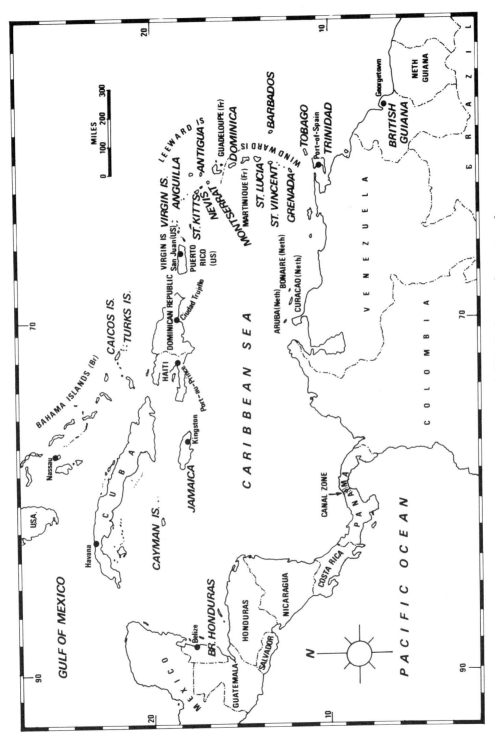

The Caribbean countries: British West Indies are shown in italic type.
This map shows the West Indies at the time of the 1950s migration (Egginton, 1957).

TESTIMONY

'West Indians never went anywhere for good, because we lived in these islands and the economic situation was so bad because these islands were ruled for Britain. We could never produce enough for ourselves to employ our people, so we've always been used to going away to work; and to begin with West Indians went to Cuba, and would stay there for two or three years but they would come back.'

'There were adverts everywhere: "Come to the mother country! The mother country needs you!" That's how I learned the opportunity was here. I felt stronger loyalty towards England. There was more emphasis there than loyalty to your own island .... It was really the mother country and being away from home wouldn't be that terrible because you would belong.'

'After being on the waiting list for two years, I wanted to do nursing in Jamaica. I decided to come to England for five years, everybody says five years .... I wanted to be a nurse and the only way I was going to make it was to get out and come to the mother country.'

'Jamaicans came here because many of them had been in the RAF .... They decided they'd come back here after the war and it was a time when people were required to build up the country ....'

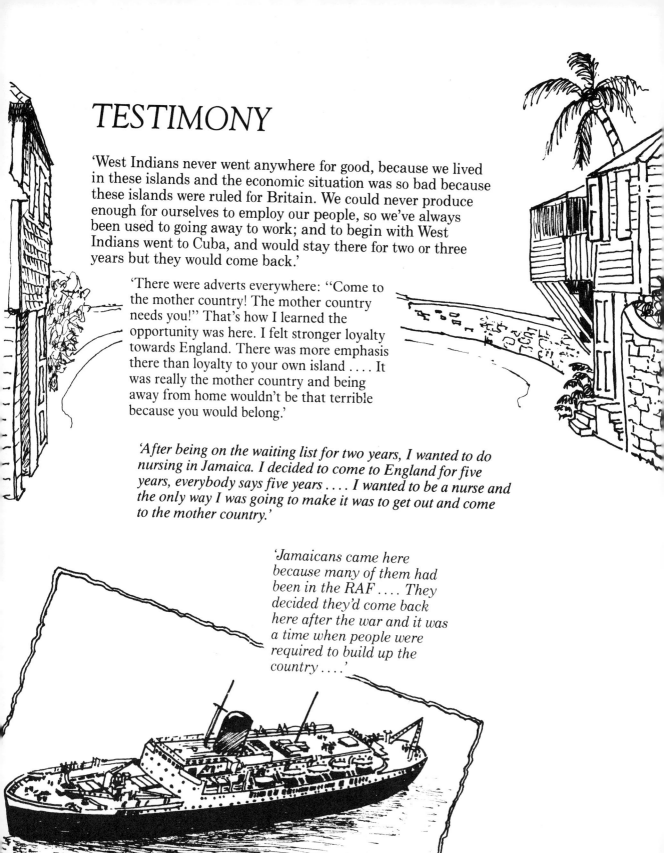

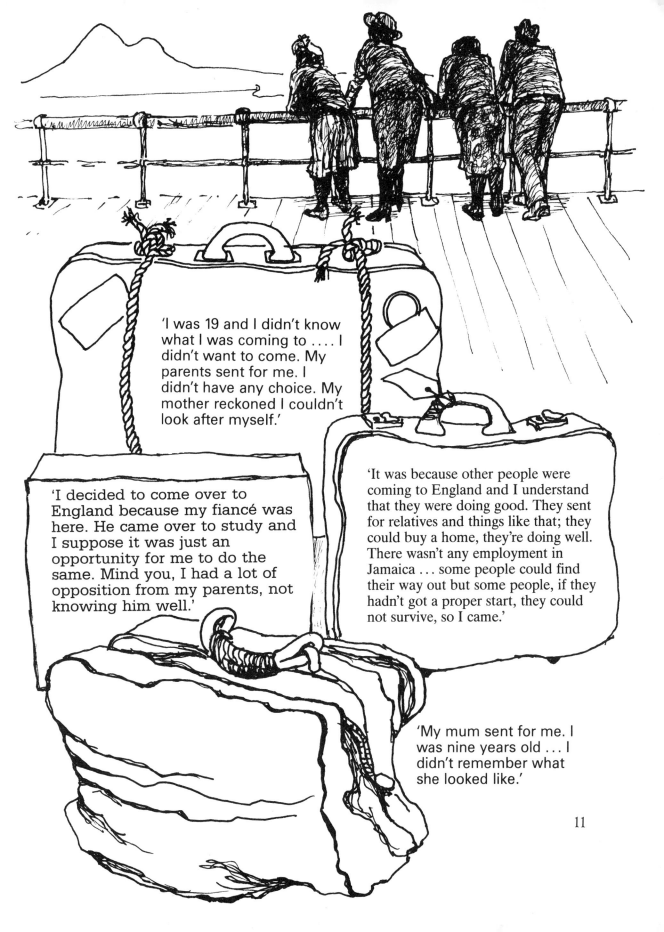

DEVELOPMENTS

1 Discuss together some of the reasons why people in the West Indies might have been attracted to England in the 1950s.

Design a poster or brochure using some of the ideas you have discussed.

Does your poster tell the whole truth? If not, discuss why.

2 Imagine you are a young person living in the West Indies in the 1950s. You want to migrate to England. Write down, as if in your diary, your reasons for wanting to go to England.

Discuss the likely reactions of other members of your family to your decision to move.

Write an account in which you and another member of the family discuss your decision to leave. You may choose any form you wish — drama, story, a poem.

3 According to Nancy Foner in her book, *Jamaica Farewell*: 'People who migrate from one country to another or from village to town, often experience dramatic changes in their way of life and in their views of the world.' Are there any circumstances in which you or a member of your family might leave the country you were born in? What dramatic changes would this bring about in your own life?

4 Find out who in your own group has had the experience of moving house. Discuss with them how they felt, what practical problems they faced, and how it changed their way of life.

Are any of the difficulties experienced by the person in your group similar to those encountered by the women who moved from the West Indies in the 1950s?

You may like to repeat this exercise by interviewing a member of your family or the local community who has moved from one place to another. If you decide to do this, you will need to discuss carefully beforehand the kinds of questions you want to ask within the interview.

2 Preparing and Parting

BACKGROUND NOTES

Raising funds

Once having decided to migrate to Britain, people had to have the means to finance the move. Preparations were needed. Funds came from a variety of sources. Some people sold their land, some used their savings, and others borrowed money from friends and relatives. Only the Barbadian government offered a state-aided system of migration to pay for the passages of those recruited to work for London Transport. These 'assisted passages' had to be repaid from the weekly earnings of the migrant in London.

Many travel agencies, however, also provided 'travel on terms'. This meant that migrants could send back most of the passage money once they were employed in Britain, provided sponsors agreed to pay if they failed to do so. (Land or livestock was often used as a guarantee.) After emigration got under way, West Indians in England sent back remittances and loans to pay for the fares of dependants, other relatives and, in some cases, friends.

Open immigration

Before the 1962 Immigration Act, which imposed restrictions on anyone who was not a dependant of persons already in Britain, there was a policy of open immigration. It was only necessary to obtain a birth certificate in order to get a passport which described West Indians as 'British subjects and citizens of the United Kingdom and Colonies'.

There were often long queues outside the passport office and many of the women recall waiting around for a long time in the scorching sun. In Kingston, Jamaica, the passport office was in busy Hanover Street and many recall the constant streams of people outside and the frustration when sometimes the supply of passports ran out.

Donald Hinds, in his moving portrait of West Indian migration, *Journey to an Illusion*, describes his own encounters with people in the days prior to his departure:

> Some of the friends and relations I had met during my last days of preparation adopted the view that it was just a matter of time before they too would be journeying to Spanish Town to get their birth certificates and lining up outside the passport office. It was a relief to be finished with queues in the boiling sun and waiting around offices.
> (Hinds, 1966, p. 36)

Preparations

At the height of migration, public notices were placed in doctors' surgeries, passport offices and other prominent places cautioning prospective migrants to arrive in Britain in suitable warm clothing so as not to endanger their health. The image of stuffing 'homemade winter woollies' into a 'cardboard suitcase' was echoed by many women as they described how they prepared to leave for England. However, all the warnings in the world cannot explain the coldness of cold to people who have never known any climate but heat. As one woman said: 'In the West Indies 60 degrees is cold.' Many women said they brought the same sort of clothes that they wore in the West Indies, but piled lots of cardigans on top.

Saying goodbye

In most people's descriptions of leaving there was usually a big send-off. This often took the form of a party the night before. Friends and relatives would come to the ports with those who were leaving to wave them goodbye. Many of the women interviewed commented on gifts that were given to them before going. These included food, clothing, items of remembrance and, most important, words of advice — 'Don't talk to strangers', 'Don't get seasick', 'Don't forget to write'.

Many of those who left were leaving close relatives behind. Often a woman left her child or children in the care of another relative until she could afford to send for them. This was an extremely emotional time for families but, as one of the women stated, members of the extended West Indian family were used to supporting each other in times of separation:

> Every time West Indian people have gone away they've left behind wives and children or husbands and children. It was inevitable if you lived in those economic conditions. It wasn't that worrying or upsetting because you're always

used to being with a lot of people. You've always lived in an extended family. When my parents left for England, I merely lived with my grandmother.

The main fears and worries were for those who were going. This was reflected by another woman who remained behind:

People were always sad to part and worried too because anything could happen in their absence. They might get sick and they'd have nobody to look after them. It was the knowing that there wouldn't be an extended family or people who had known you all your life that worried people remaining behind the most.

The journey

In 1948 the S.S. *Empire Windrush* brought the first large group of migrants to Britain from the West Indies. They numbered 492 in all and the majority of them were young, male, semi-skilled and skilled workers from Jamaica. By 1953 there were still only three ships — two French and one British — but by 1955 there were thirteen ships on the run. These ships made forty sailings during that year. The S.S. *Auriga* and the M.S. *Andrea Gritti* (see p. 4) were two of the ships that sailed this route carrying well over 1000 people on board as it picked up passengers from several West Indian islands.

The passage usually cost between £75 and £85 in the mid-1950s. £85 would provide cabin accommodation for six, while £75, known as the 'dormitory fare', would provide a cabin to be shared with about twenty others. The time of the journey (approximately eighteen days) varied depending upon whether the ship was to go direct to England or, as many of the Italian liners did, go by sea to Genoa. After that the travellers would have to take a train from Genoa to Calais and then cross the Channel to Dover.

Accounts of the journey to Britain vary from descriptions of the voyage as being 'pleasant' and 'quite nice' to more horrific accounts of insanitary conditions, sea sickness and bad food.

There were also a few chartered air flights operating at the time. The average fare for flying was £85 (see p. 4).

TESTIMONY

'My mother wasn't too sure that I should come so she gave me a lot of advice ... if you don't like it over there you can always come back.'

'My mother took quite a lot of persuading before she eventually gave in. I was the first daughter to leave home, so you can imagine how terribly upset everybody was. My family came down to see me off. The first thing my mother said to me was not to get involved with anyone on the boat. They warned me about being seasick, because it was the first time I'd travelled; that I should write to them at every port we stayed; as soon as I arrived I had to cable them to let them know that I had arrived safely.'

'They had a big party the night we left and loads of friends and relatives came to wave us goodbye. I promised to come back to see them in five years. It was a very emotional time.'

'My sister came with me to the airport. My father couldn't bear the thought of coming, it was too painful to part. So we said goodbye at home. He didn't say much; he was lost for words, overwhelmed.'

'Once I decided to leave I had to get my documents in order, I knew I was going to leave my family, but ... if you have to go you just have to go; once your money's paid you just have to go.'

'I sent Sharon to the shop to get a cake and when she came back I was gone.'

'I was very sad leaving my kids behind, very sad. But y'know since I had that plan to send for them, I knew it wouldn't be too long before I see them again.'

'Although you left your children behind, I was a child left behind. I wasn't at all worried or upset because you have always lived in the extended family. I merely lived with my grandmother. I wasn't worried or upset. I just got a bit fed up with my grandmother.'

'It wasn't anything final. I mean they were leaving home for two or three years, they weren't leaving for good and I think they were always planning. They would say goodbye and I'll see you in two years' time.'

DEVELOPMENTS

1 You have decided to leave Jamaica in order to get a job in England in the 1950s. Discuss how you might raise the money for the trip. (See p. 4 for the fares.)

Give an account of how you tried to persuade your parents that your intended trip was a realistic and necessary step to take.

Many of your friends and relatives have given you gifts and mementos to remember them by. Describe some of them and their importance to you.

2 Imagine you are the parent of one of the women who came to England when she was young. Her ship has just left. Discuss how you feel.

Write a poem, an extract from your diary or a letter to a friend about the parting.

3 The idea of taking a journey is one of the great themes in the myths and literature of all peoples. Find an example from your own reading. Compare and contrast this experience of travel with the West Indian experience of migration.

4 Using the women's testimony as your source material, write a newspaper account that might have appeared in the *Jamaican Gleaner* in the late 1950s.

Describe the scenes at the port as families and friends say goodbye to each other.

3 First Impressions

BACKGROUND NOTES

By the mid-1950s a lot of publicity was being given to the arrival of the 'boat-trains' at the big London termini (Victoria, Paddington, Waterloo), carrying the newly-arrived West Indians from the ports into London. Newspaper reporters, feature writers and photographers usually covered the arrivals showing an assortment of pictures with captions describing the West Indians with their 'calypso flamboyance' and 'indifference' to the cold air of the 'frosty English winter'. The feelings described by many of the people who came during those times gives quite a different impression.

Initial responses

Many of those who were interviewed about their arrival easily recalled their first day in Britain. They give vivid and detailed descriptions of their first journey through Britain from the ports into London. Many commented on the bleak industrial landscapes — terraced houses with chimneys seemed to them more like factories than homes. Some recall the immediate feeling of being isolated blacks in a predominantly white country and the shock of seeing English people doing manual work: 'white women scrubbing concrete steps' and 'white men sweeping the streets'. Everyone commented upon the cold. They had no idea how cold it would be. Some arrived in the middle of winter in lightweight clothes, but many friends and relatives came prepared with a spare coat when they were met.

Arrival at the London stations

None of the train stations was equipped to cope with the large numbers of new arrivals, many of whom were forced to wait around for hours before being collected by friends and relatives. There were joyful reunions and for some a swift journey to accommodation that had been previously arranged. Others were not so fortunate. Some had the addresses of friends, but many of these were confined to surnames and streets (e.g. Mrs Smith, King Street, London). Others had been told that it was best to take a taxi upon arrival and had to be dissuaded from taking taxis to Manchester or Birmingham, not realizing how far distances were within Britain. Some said they sensed 'annoyance' on the faces of porters, cabbies and policemen as they made enquiries or asked for directions.

According to Donald Hinds, it was not uncommon for twelve people to turn out to meet only one migrant, but not all who turned out were related to the newcomer:

> Some went out of curiosity. They hoped to meet an old school friend or even a relation. . . . Others were landlords or front men for white organizations which were buying up the more dilapidated houses and letting them to the newcomers for high rents.
> (Hinds, 1966, p. 52)

People left stranded

There were many people who came from the West Indies without any idea of what they were to do when they got off the train. Wives and girlfriends hoping to meet their men folk who had come previously were sometimes left stranded. Edward Scobie, in his study of the history of black people in Britain, *Black Britannia*, describes the despair and disappointment that some people had to face amidst the chaos:

> Eyes searched everywhere for relations and friends who were supposed to be there to meet them. Some were disappointed and lost and had to depend on the bounty of British officialdom. Spivs, wide boys and 'sharks' of both races circulated in the crowds wanting to prey on the unfortunate ones.
> (Scobie, 1972, p. 197)

The authorities were finally so disturbed by these huge reception committees that they would announce the boat-train was arriving at one station and switch it without any notice to another.

TESTIMONY

'We landed at Southampton. My husband was meeting me.... When I saw him I felt overwhelmed ... it was a feeling of total confusion having to go through immigration ... and all the people around you that you didn't know ... I felt utterly despairing. It was a feeling of total confusion because I suddenly realized I'd arrived, I'd left home and I arrived here.'

'There were curious onlookers standing around looking; anxious black people and curious white people.'

'It was a cold, cold November day. People were so cold. I wanted to turn around and go back; it had all been a horrible mistake.'

'We landed at Gatwick airport. There were lots of people waiting for their relatives. I felt lost and alone ... it was a mixed feeling. I was supposed to meet my sister but somehow we got lost and I had to take a taxi down to Birmingham.'

'We took the train from Plymouth to Victoria Station. It was night when we came there. It was cold.... The first thing I noticed, I look on all the houses and I say what a lot of factories.'

'I was on the train and when I looked out through the window and see all these little houses, and outside is so black, I said to somebody, "When are we going to reach England?"'

'My friend came to meet me at Waterloo. The scene was just a lot of people. Everybody who come off the train and who come to meet relatives. So it was just a big crowd of people.'

'One of the things that shocked me was looking around and seeing English people doing manual work. It seemed so depressing the picture that I built up in my mind. It wasn't that I thought it was the golden land but the streets, the space, the houses all capped together and no spaces and chimneys. It seemed very dull.'

'My husband come to meet me, everything was strange. Nowhere to live, nowhere to sleep, nowhere... nobody want to know you.'

'I was wearing a tailored woollen suit and my cousin met me with a coat.... Before I got that coat, I was so cold, Oh God.... We took a taxi and I remember how friendly I thought the taxi driver was but the accent, the strange accent.'

DEVELOPMENTS

1   Here is an excerpt from a fictional account of West Indians arriving in Britain by the Barbadian writer, George Lamming, from his novel, *The Emigrants*:

> Here pavement. Over there luggage. Beyond crowds. Vague and ragged waiting to greet friends. You can't see them clearly because things get thicker like a blacksmith's shop after something has gone wrong. No blaze. No fire. Just a thick choking mass of cloud. The men bend to read the names. Beyond the people crowd like refugees. As though something had happened outside to frighten them into hiding! Only these voices speak clearly. The strange ones. The men working on the platform. The others talk as though they were choked. Weak. Frightened. They said it wouldn't be so cold. So cold ... so frightened ... so frightened ... home ... go ... to go back ... home ... only because ... this like ... no ... home ... other reason ... because ... like this ... frightened ... alone ... the whole place ... goes up up up and over up and over curling falling ... up ... over to heaven ... down to ... hell up an' over ... thick ... sick ... thick ... sick ... up ... cold ... so ... frightened ... no ... don't ... don't tremble ... no ... not ... frightened ... no ... alone ... no
> (Lamming, 1980, p. 122–3)

How does this fictional description compare with the women's accounts of arrival? Using information from the women's testimony, write down the thoughts, in the way George Lamming has done, that might have been passing through their minds.

2   Write either a poem or a story or draw a picture called 'First Impressions'. Describe what struck you most on first arriving in Britain. Remember things like the weather, houses, the space, other people.

3   You are about to write a letter home in order to reassure your parents that everything is well. Discuss with members of your group what you might include in the letter.

Write an extract from your 'honest diary' (it wouldn't be read by anyone else) called: 'What I really feel about being in England'.

4 Housing

BACKGROUND NOTES

Finding a place

Many West Indian migrants found it extremely difficult to find accommodation when they arrived in Britain. Before the Second World War the housing situation in Britain was in a serious state and slum clearances had to be postponed with the outbreak of war in 1939. During the war 223,000 homes were totally destroyed by German bombs and rockets. This added to the long list of people who had been waiting for borough or county councils to house them. (In 1955, the London Borough of Lambeth had 10,000 families on the housing waiting-list.)

Having just arrived in Britain, West Indian migrants didn't qualify for council houses. (Each borough had different regulations, e.g. in Lambeth you had to live in the borough for three years before you could qualify.) Moreover, there was a general unwillingness among white landlords and landladies to take black tenants. They were widely rejected as tenants of advertised flats and lodgings on the basis of what was known then as the *colour bar*. 'So sorry — no coloureds, no children', 'European Only', 'White Only' signs dotted the pages of advertisements and local notice boards (this became illegal after the 1968 Race Relations Act). There was also often a *colour tax* which was a term used to describe the higher rents and higher house prices imposed on black migrants.

No special provision was made to enable the newly-arrived migrant to find accommodation and most West Indians were left to find their own living space. Many of the women who were interviewed spoke of the humiliation they felt when a door was slammed shut in their face after they had enquired about accommodation. This was particularly difficult for women with children. Most women began life in Britain living in the few boarding and lodging houses that would accept them.

Buying a house

With good rented accommodation so hard to obtain many started to save their money in order to buy houses. As soon as enough was saved for a down payment the search for a property would begin. Many people were exploited by estate agents who channelled migrants into less saleable districts of towns and cities with inferior accommodation. Others could only afford short-term leases but bought up deteriorating property as a temporary solution. Often they managed to pay the mortgage off by letting available rooms in the house to other newly-arrived migrants and later bought freehold and longer leasehold houses.

Many women were responsible for the decision to try and purchase property at the expense of saving to return home to the West Indies. As one of the women involved in the Motherland Project stated: 'In this country the women came and

they decided they couldn't live in these terrible conditions and so this saving to go home in two years had to go because they needed houses to live in . . .'.

Living conditions

Most people lived in one furnished room when they first arrived in Britain. In the Brixton area of London the average rent for a small room was about 25—30 shillings (£1.25p—£1.50p) per week in the years between 1955—1958. Fifty shillings (£2.50p) was the charge for a large room. This usually included a bed, table, dresser, kitchen cabinet, wardrobe and chair, joint use of toilet and bathroom with the other tenants in the house and a change of bedlinen and towels once a fortnight. There was often a gas cooker on the landing shared by about four families each paying 4—6 shillings a week for gas. Many women who traditionally did the cooking for their families found this difficult to cope with. The rent was often much higher than most English people were paying for the same accommodation. Many were reluctant to take the case of their high rents to the rent tribunal. However, those that did found their rents cut by as much as 50 per cent.

The relationship between the women and their landladies and landlords was a crucial factor governing their living conditions. There were often restrictions such as a ten o'clock evening curfew and restricted visiting. Some were charged extra for use of heating and lighting; others were refused use of some electrical appliances.

For some women who often had sole responsibility for childcare there were problems with children making noise. Some commented on the constant nagging they were faced with and the fact that they felt as if they were being watched all the time. In many houses children were not allowed, so that if a woman was obviously pregnant she was immediately evicted. However, a landlady/lord could evict a tenant for any reason. More than one of the interviewees came home to find all her belongings out on the street.

TESTIMONY

'I was looking for a better reception towards us ... no vacancy ... I wouldn't have left Jamaica if I'd known.'

'I lost days from work looking for a room.... The situation was very bad. I felt very bitter.'

'We encountered lots and lots of problems looking for somewhere to live ... the white folk didn't want to know, sometimes they just close the door in your face. Even with blacks, blacks didn't want anybody with children.'

'We knew it was cold, but we didn't believe it would be so cold as how it was. I thought when you come in the house you really warm, you understand? I thought that way, but it was nothing like that because if you don't have a little coal you can't light no fire.'

'Them rent you a room, but you can't do anything. Sometimes you had to hide the iron. There's certain times I had to wake up about five o'clock and I do a little ironing. That time the children were small and I wasn't going to work but no light — no light during the whole day. No visitors, nobody can come look for you.'

'They didn't want neighbours to know that they're renting a room; all the curtains were the same; they want the neighbours to think it's all one house. ... If you buy a chair they give you notice to go.'

'When we gone to work and come back everything was thrown out. Everything that we possess was outside ... outside on the ground.... We can't get back in. And in those days we can't go to the police.'

'We had to put lights on to change the baby. The landlord said we had to pay extra.'

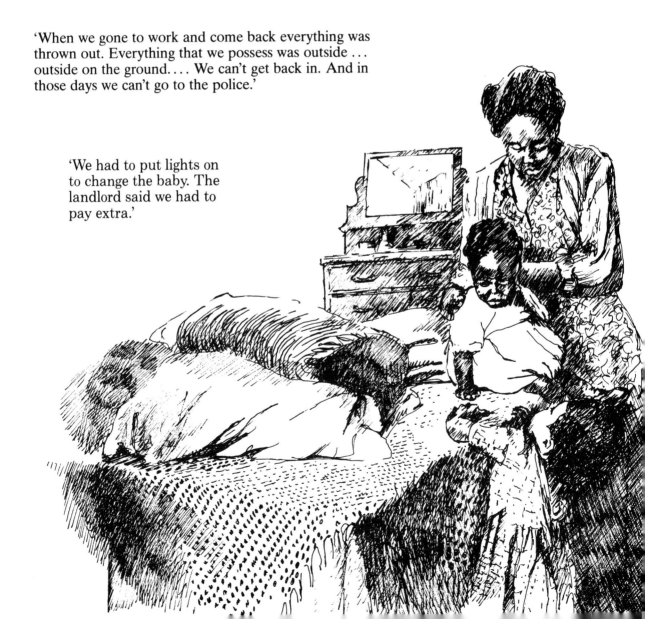

DEVELOPMENTS

1   The *West Indian Gazette*, started in March 1958, was the first newspaper of its kind in Britain. Edited by Claudia Jones, it reported on events at home and also within the West Indian community in Britain. It aimed right from the start to take a strong line against racial discrimination.

Imagine you are the editor of the *West Indian Gazette*. Write an editorial for your new paper which you hope West Indian people will read. The purpose of the editorial is to highlight the difficulties that people are having with regard to accommodation.

2   Discuss in small groups the genuine complaints and grievances that the women had about their living conditions. Go on to discuss the ways in which they might approach the landlady/lord about one of their grievances.

In pairs, work out a scene in which one of the tenants meets the landlady/lord. You may write this down as a playscript. Act it out through improvisation, or write it in story form.

3   Imagine you are an adult member of the following family living in one room with a kitchen and bath shared with three other families:

> a child of two needing constant attention;
> a child of seven who attends school between 9 am and 3.30 pm, who needs to be taken to school and fetched;
> one parent who works a shift from 8 am — 5 pm;
> one parent who works a shift from 2 pm — 10 pm.

Explain some of the problems this routine imposes upon you and how you might have to rely on other people to help you resolve these.

5 Earning a Living

BACKGROUND NOTES

As we have seen, thousands of West Indians came to Britain, having been recruited to work for London Transport, British Railways and the National Health Service. As Claudia Jones, editor of the *West Indian Gazette* during that period, wrote:

> Throughout Britain, the West Indian contribution to its economy is undoubted. As building workers, carpenters, as nurses, doctors and on hospital staffs, in factories, on the transportation system and railway depots and stations, West Indians are easily evidenced.
> (Jones, 1978, p. 34)

England had been presented as a country with more than enough work to go round. However, although many migrants obtained work immediately, some women recall that it took as long as eight months to find a job. As one woman said, she was often given the same excuse by firms who had advertised job vacancies: 'We've got jobs, but we can't give them all to your people'.

They were recruited into those sections of industry requiring cheap, unskilled labour and into service industries. Migrant workers, particularly female migrant workers, were at the bottom of the pile as far as employment was concerned. Once a job was found, conditions of work were generally unattractive with low pay, long and often unsocial hours, and poor prospects.

Discrimination and racist abuse were part of everyday reality for many. Some West Indian workers had to struggle to be accepted in their jobs. For example, even though Barbados had an agreement with London Transport to train workers, there were battles waged for upgrading West Indian workers, for their right to work in booking offices, and for West Indian women to be employed as bus conductresses in the early years of migration.

Few West Indian applicants were accepted for clerical jobs or work such as shop assistants, counter assistants or waitresses. Many employers justified this on the grounds that 'the public might not like it'. There was also a 10 per cent quota on the employment of West Indian workers in many factories at the time.

Special induction courses were set up in factories especially for the 'newcomers'. Many found these insulting and humiliating. On these courses the 'newcomers' were issued with a set of rules which emphasized the importance of 'adapting' and 'behaving' like everybody else (see *Pointers*, Lesson 5, p. 115).

Women workers

Many women came to Britain as independent workers leaving their families behind. Some were recruited directly in the West Indies, some heard of jobs

through friends who had gone before them, and others found their jobs on arrival. For many of the women, coming from a rural environment, it was the first time they had worked for a wage in an urban industrial economy.

They worked long hours for little pay. According to a report in the journal *Race Today*: 'The average wage was about £6 per week compared to white women who during the same period were receiving an average wage of £8 a week.' (Race Today Women, 1975, p. 110). On this wage, they not only maintained themselves and their children who were with them, but sent money home to their children and relatives in the Caribbean.

Many women went into hospital work when they arrived in Britain. The relationship between black women and the nursing profession is traced in another article in *Race Today*:

> Nursing is a 'caring profession', and traditionally the work of women — to be of service not only to their own men and children, but to other people's. No woman is more identified with service work than black women, especially the black women with a slave or colonial past.
> (Black Womens Group, 1974, p. 226)

Most of the women interviewed for the Motherland Project had some experience of hospital work in Britain as either nurses or auxiliaries. They spoke of the hostility they experienced from patients and other hospital staff. Even when training as nurses, the women were discouraged from taking the SRN examination, which allowed them opportunity for promotion, in favour of the SEN qualification — a shorter course with lower status. As one of the women explained:

> A lot of us fell for that [doing SEN instead of SRN]. If we were given a chance at the time to sit the test to do SRN a lot of us would have got through. We were sort of cheap labour really.

TESTIMONY

'I went to a hospital in Fulham, as an auxiliary. It was mostly black people. Some of the patients were nice and some of them were horrible, but they were so sick ... they don't want you to come near, they don't want you to touch them. It makes you feel bitter but you want the job so you have to stick it because if you tell anything to them they will complain to matron and you will get the sack. You don't know where you are going to have the next one so you just have to stick it ... you just carry on with the job.'

'I came from Jamaica straight into the nurses' home; the reception was very good.... We didn't have much trouble with the white nurses very little. We sort of didn't mix you see. We kept ourselves to ourselves. The nursing tutors didn't like us — or it would appear as if they didn't like us, because we were given very low marks no matter how hard we try. So that made us try harder....'

'Yes the black girls used to get very low marks.... I never used to write home and tell my dad. Oh no, I wouldn't do that because he'd be worried out of his mind.... No, I always tell him I'm happy.'

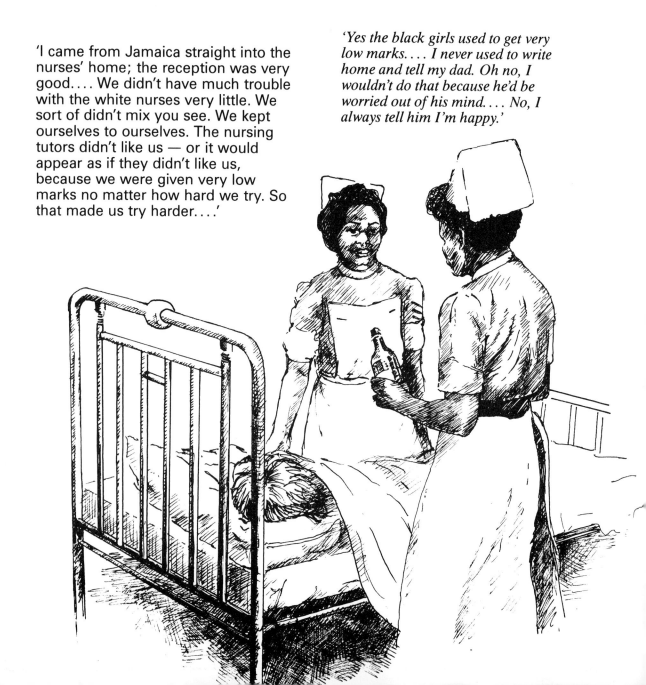

'We had to start work at six.... I had to catch the bus at half-past five. It was so hard in the winter. When you go in the factory in the morning it was so cold, ever so cold.'

'When I came to England in 1958 it was very hard for me to get a job. One of the reasons was because I was black.... I could do any job, but when I came into the country I was made to understand what it is like, you see, so I was seeking a job in a factory.'

'My first job was at Blackfriars, but it didn't last very long just temporary. It wasn't at all easy to find a job. That was in 1957, I come over in November and I didn't get a job until February because I didn't know the place so well. At that time anything I'd get I'd take it ... I think it was easier for a man to find a job at that time....'

'I went to Peak Freans that used to have loads of part-time jobs and this woman said to me "We've got jobs yes, but we can't give it to all your people." I was surprised but I didn't take it as racist then.... I thought it was reasonable for her to say that.'

'I think most of the women who came over are really strong. They didn't know what they were going to find. Most West Indians came from a rural background, they'd never seen a factory.'

DEVELOPMENTS

1   The women faced two kinds of racial discrimination. First, there was the feeling of personal dislike or uneasiness in their presence which was directed against them by other individuals. Second, there was the way in which the rules, traditions and conventions of various institutions operated against them. This second kind of discrimination exerted a particular influence at work. Find an example, from the testimony and background notes, of each kind of discrimination.

Discuss how it affected the women's lives. Could the same thing happen today?

2   You are one of the women who has come over for better job opportunities in the 1950s. Now you feel you have been treated unfairly as a result of a particular incident that has occurred at work. Write a letter to your employer describing your grievance.

3   Since there was no legislation covering discrimination at work in the 1950s, what few initiatives there were had to be taken on an individual basis.

Imagine that you are an employer seriously concerned with giving a fair share to all. What measures might you take to ensure that West Indian people, as a group, were not at a disadvantage when seeking a job and that their conditions of service were acceptable at your place of work?

6 Childcare

BACKGROUND NOTES

In the West Indies childcare was rarely a serious problem. Grandmothers, aunties, sisters and cousins often lived closely together and felt a strong sense of mutual responsibility. On arrival in England, however, few migrant women had their mothers or close relatives at hand. Invariably they were forced to take sole responsibility for caring for their children.

In post-war Britain married women of all classes with small children were pressurized to stay at home. Many childcare 'experts' in the 1950s (see, for example, John Bowlby, 1953) claimed that proper mothering was only possible if the mother did not go out to work. (Most of these claims were later disproved.) As a result of this belief there was a reduced provision of childcare facilities such as day nurseries. In 1951 the Ministry of Health recommended that day care provision be refused to any woman who was going to work solely to supplement the family income.

In spite of these beliefs about women and childcare, West Indian women coming to Britain at this time were expected to work. After all, that is why they had been encouraged to migrate. Many of them were wives and mothers as well as workers. Nevertheless, the British government did not increase its expenditure on childcare facilities to accommodate the new work-forces. With little state provision for childcare, women were left to find their own facilities.

Men whose shifts were different from those of their wives often cared for children. Women, too, who often worked different shifts helped each other out by looking after one another's children. Private nurseries were expensive and there were few places in state nurseries. Some women decided not to work when their children were very small and others worked part time. Most women involved in the Motherland Project agreed that childcare responsibilities made it difficult to work and limited the kinds of jobs they applied for. At some time or other, they had all given their children over to the care of childminders when they were at work.

Childminding

In 1948, the Nurseries and Childminders Regulation Act was passed which for the first time required minimum standards for people caring for other people's children and being paid for it. However, in the 1950s the regulations regarding registered childminders were neither well known nor effectively enforced. There were many unlicensed minders caring for children in conditions that were totally unsuitable. Many women were very anxious about the care their children were receiving; some spoke of how they worried at work all day and many discovered that their children were being mistreated. Some of the most common complaints were about unsafe and insanitary surroundings: babies not being fed, washed or changed enough, and the number of children being cared for by one person in a small space. Even when the facilities were adequate, it was expensive. On average it cost 20–30 shillings per week for one child. Some women eventually took up childminding themselves as an alternative to going out to work.

Working women

The lot of working women with young children was an exhausting one. Although some husbands helped out in the house the major responsibilities for the home usually rested with the woman whether she worked or not. It was the women who left the children with the minder before work and fetched them afterwards. Few of them had much time for rest at the end of the day:

> You come in from work. You wash the nappies, cook the dinner. Then you have to watch that they don't turn over the paraffin heater. It's just a day-to-day thing.

This is the voice of one of the women who was interviewed. She had to live in one room with her husband and two children when she came to England. Like many of the women we spoke to she felt that it was difficult raising children in a large city with few open spaces and nowhere for them to play. She found this so different to the situation in the West Indies where mothers felt more secure about their children's safety.

This sense of security about the well-being of children in the West Indies is described by Margaret Prescod-Roberts in an account of her own migration from Barbados in *Bringing It All Back Home*:

> If you live in a village in an extended family you know that if your child's outside somewhere, someone will be looking out for her. If your child is out in the street and the neighbour down the road sees your child in some mess, that woman is going to take the responsibility of dealing with that child.
> (Prescod-Roberts, 1980, p. 28)

Most women just didn't have the same confidence about their children playing out in the streets of London.

TESTIMONY

'After you carry your baby and you come to give them at morning time you don't know what's happening; they just take them from you. You sit in work worrying all day what's happening to them.'

'It was hard bringing up two children in one room. You get up in the morning, take them down to the childminder at 6 o'clock in the morning. No choice you have to.... It was rough, there was no other way. I had to start at 7. You have to work.'

'A woman said to me one day, "What a lovely baby, oh she's nice and sweet. Where do you take her?" I told her and she says, "Lord have mercy, you mustn't take your baby down there 'cause she puts them downstairs on the basement floor." So I went down to the basement, I pushed past the woman and I looked at all the pickney on the floor that had been brought there in the morning time.'

'When my children were younger, I couldn't work really because I find out that the lady that looked after them wasn't looking after them as how I thought she should. So I give up work, but things got very difficult for me.'

'One day I left work early and when I knocked on the door, you could see this woman was frightened. It was the same as when I took the baby in the morning. The baby was in the pushchair the same way, her coat on her the same way, sleeping in the pushchair.... She never take out the baby.'

'My husband wasn't working. The job that he was doing was finished.... I thought, well, I could go back to work and he could look after the baby. He looked after her until he get a job.'

'I stayed home until they were about five. I never do full-time work when they were very young. Their upbringing was very restricted compared to what I had.... There's not much here for young children really.'

'I gave out Linda for about three years next door. One day a white lady said to me, "Linda is better off with you". So you could read between the lines. She was the shopkeeper, so I packed it in.... It's no good idea to give your children out.'

DEVELOPMENTS

1   Imagine you are a West Indian parent in the 1950s. You are about to go to work but before you do you have to take your child to be looked after for the day. It is the first time your child will have met the childminder. Discuss what you must say to prepare your child for the visit.

Describe the scene between mother and child before they set off.

2   Childminding is a difficult and highly-skilled task. Many of the women who were childminding had to run their own homes, looking after their own family as well as taking care of other people's children. This was a difficult and time consuming job.

Imagine you were a childminder during the 1950s. How might you have organized your day in such a way as to meet the needs (in terms of feeding, entertaining and overseeing) the children you were minding, while at the same time fulfilling your own household responsibilities?

Starting at 7 am when the first child is delivered, outline your routine for the whole day until 8 pm when the last child is collected.

3   The following is a description from Buchi Emecheta's book *Second Class Citizen*, in which Adah, a Nigerian living in London, describes a surprise visit she made in the middle of the day to the minder of her children, Vicky and Titi:

> She ran out and saw her children. She stood there, her knees shaking and burst into tears. Vicky was busy pulling rubbish out of the bin and Titi was washing her hands and face with the water leaking from the toilet. When they saw her, they ran to her, and Adah noticed that Vicky had no nappy on.... Adah bundled the children into their pushchair and took them to the children's officer at Malden Road. After all, Trudy was a registered babyminder, whatever that was supposed to mean.
> (Emecheta, 1977, p. 57)

Describe the scene in which Adah confronts the children's officer who was responsible for registering childminders throughout the borough.

7 Relationships with Men

BACKGROUND NOTES

In the 1950s in Britain there was a fairly strict division between what was expected of men and of women: women were expected to be good mothers and homemakers and men to be family providers. We have seen how the British attitude towards working mothers was responsible for the poor provision of childcare facilities and how this placed West Indian mothers in an extremely difficult position.

It was difficult, too, for West Indian men to fulfil their expected role of 'breadwinner'. This was largely due to the racial discrimination which confined so many of them to low-status and poorly-paid jobs. Many of the women who were interviewed spoke of how their husbands had changed as a result of these pressures. Couples living in this insecure migrant situation found that their relationships broke down.

Many of the women interviewed believed that this breakdown occurred more rapidly because of the lack of emotional ties provided by the kind of extended family structure common in the West Indies. Back home all members of the family would have supported one another at times of stress. In Britain, the couples were often isolated; neither friends nor relatives were nearby.

For some women being left on their own with children strengthened their resolve to maintain their traditional values and transmit these to their children. Many women developed a more independent lifestyle and tended to relate more to one another than to men.

Those who stayed with their original male partners discovered that their relationships were changing. Women were not dependent on their husbands for financial support as many had been in the West Indies. They felt freer to express dissatisfaction and make demands. As wage earners women felt a new sense of power in relation to their men: 'Here you work for yourself. In this country we do as we like. I have my own pay packet and don't wait on my husband for money.'

In Britain many of the men tended to share more household responsibilities than they ever did before. There was still a major division of labour — women doing cleaning, cooking, childcare and men tending to do decorating and household repairs. However, when men's shifts were different from those of their wives they often looked after their children. This need to share roles and responsibilities is described in the journal *Race Today*:

> If a woman does shift work at a factory and is away from home between 2pm and 10pm, she is not available that week to cook and serve the evening meal at home. The consequence is that the division of labour within the family has to undergo some change.
> (Race Today Women, 1975, p. 99)

In Nancy Foner's study of Jamaican migrants in London, *Jamaica Farewell*, she stressed that when women are wage earners they are treated more like partners. According to her study, there was a tendency for couples to share more and go out together more than they had done in the West Indies. However, there were still some things they did separately: men tended to go to pubs and parties together and women attended church regularly with their female friends and relatives.

TESTIMONY

'We come from a society where men were always the providers.... I suppose that would create a lot of problems because the women are working here. They're more independent. It's going to create a conflict 'cause some ladies work more than their husbands and the husbands resent that.'

'After being given the chance of doing SRN I met my husband. It was love at first sight and I didn't stay on to do a third year.... We are still together.... We could only face the things we had to face because we had certain values.'

'He comes in and he doesn't even give me the housekeeping money. He comes in when he wants his food and says where is the dinner ... after you've been working all day. You might as well live on your own.'

'It's just how the older women were brought up to try and see if they can make it work.... So the responsibility of keeping the marriage together actually rests solely on you.'

'He's lucky that when he had past through all these things he had somebody like me to stand with him. 'Cause a lot of ladies would have chickened out and scattered.'

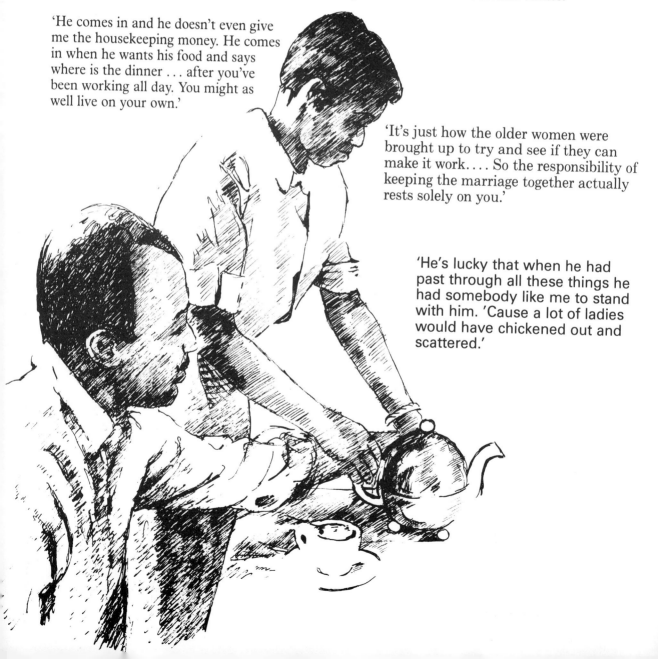

'It was the 19th of October grey and cold. I wondered how I'd ever be able to stand it because I loved sunny days. I was glad to see him and be with him.'

'When I got home from work in the evening I found he wasn't there. I didn't see most of his things in the room; he didn't leave any message.'

'I think relationships broke down because of the pressure of the long working hours ... you work in Jamaica but the weather is different, you're among friends and family, but here you feel isolated. ... In the West Indies, you don't have to go out to work; you can just stay at home and have your children. It's a completely different way of running a marriage.'

'I don't see why you should sit and let a man get you down. I mean, if you sit and depend upon a man in this day and age you'll always want them around. Everything that I've done I've done by myself.'

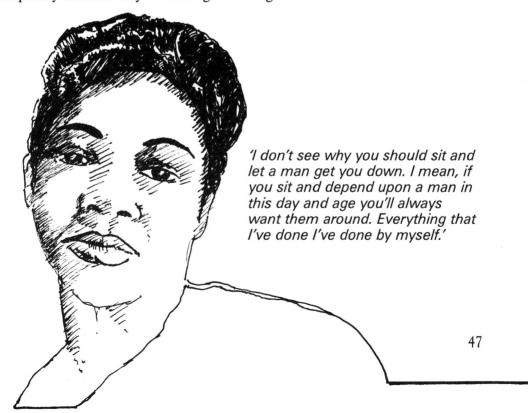

DEVELOPMENTS

1   You have been separated from your spouse for some time and are reunited in England. What were your feelings as you were waiting for the boat-train to arrive? What were the first words spoken?

Describe meeting your partner off the boat-train.

2   Giving examples from the women's testimony show how, for many of the women who came to Britain, migration changed their relationships with their husbands.

Describe a scene between two women in which they explain to each other some of the changes in their relationship with their husbands since they came to Britain.

3   Some relationships lasted. The following poem by the black American writer, Alice Walker, is a tribute to the relationship between her own parents. 'Good night, Willie Lee, I'll see you in the morning' is a sad poem but also celebratory:

> Looking down into my father's
> dead face
> for the last time
> my mother said without
> tears, without smiles
> without regrets
> but with civility
> 'Good night, Willie Lee, I'll see you
> in the morning.'
> And it was then I knew that the
>   healing
> Of all our wounds
> is forgiveness
> that permits a promise
> of our return
> at the end.
> (Walker, 1975, p. 53)

Imagine you are Willie Lee's widow. Write an account that looks back on the relationship with your husband, highlighting the good times and the bad times.

8 Responses to the 'New Community'

BACKGROUND NOTES

Migrant workers to Britain have always had to face a certain amount of hostility from the 'host society'. According to Sheila Patterson's study of the Brixton community in the 1950s, this British reluctance to accept outsiders was intensified by the fact that in this case the newcomers were black. Her description of the West Indian migrant as the 'supreme and ultimate stranger' gives some indication of the white community's response to the newcomers.

Many of the women interviewed spoke of how they were made to feel different in England: many used the word 'shock' to describe their initial response to the 'new community'. They were brought up to respect 'the English way of life' and had hoped to live and work in Britain as equals. They had been taught about British history, the Queen, the Constitution, and had been led to believe that they would be welcome. Many of them were, therefore, surprised to discover that English people knew little, if anything, about them. The comments and questions of the English people they met were irritating and sometimes offensive. Some genuinely believed that West Indians had lived in trees or worn only pieces of cloth around their waist at home. Even those who were less ignorant could not distinguish between West Indians and West Africans. They asked questions which clearly showed that they did not know where the islands of the West Indies were located (e.g. 'Is British Guiana the same as Ghana?') nor did they realize that, for most, English was their first language (e.g. 'How did you manage to learn English so quickly?').

Racism

Generations of people in Britain grew up in a period in which their country ruled vast areas of the world that included hundreds of millions of black people ('The British Empire'). They learned that it was good to be British and unfortunate to be black. In their booklet *Patterns of Racism*, the Institute of Race Relations shows how this notion of 'white racial superiority' was present in all aspects of British life:

> It was there in the language, the literature and the history of white civilization. It was there in the schools, in the workplaces and pubs, in the language and thinking of governments. Infants were taught it through their nursery tales, children through their school books and comics. And adults went on believing it. . . .
> (Institute of Race Relations, 1982, p. 39)

It is important to understand how these ideas have affected the ways in which British society is organized when we look at some of the individual acts of racialist oppression and abuse that West Indians had to face.

The 'Colour Bar' was the phrase used to describe the way in which black people in Britain were barred from many important areas of social life when they first arrived. As early as July 1949, the popular magazine *Picture Post* ran a major feature entitled 'Is there a British Colour Bar?' and found that indeed there was.

Instances of rejection and refusals at hotels, pubs, dance halls and restaurants were widely reported. Most of the contacts between the two communities tended to occur in public places — on the buses, over the counter, at the post office. Many of the women we interviewed described the pain and tension they felt in some of these situations because of the racial prejudice they encountered.

Nottingham, Notting Hill, 1958 and 1959

One of the most terrible experiences for the West Indian community in Britain was the racist attacks on black people that occurred in Nottingham and in the Notting Hill area of London throughout the summer of 1958 and later in 1959. Right-wing extremist groups instigated much of the violence with slogans such as 'We'll get the Blacks', 'Act Now' and 'K.B.W.' ('Keep Britain White'). Attacks on black people and their property were made indiscriminately — on men, women and children, on the old and the young.

Dilip Hiro, in his book *Black British, White British*, describes the change that occurred throughout the black community in the way its members perceived their presence in England after Nottingham and Notting Hill:

> They were made to realize that they were not 'overseas British' now living in Britain, but were black men and women living in a white society. With this, a new chapter in the racial history of Britain began.
> (Hiro, 1971, p. 40)

This change of attitude is summed up by one of the women we interviewed about the impact of the summer of 1958 on her life:

> After that I never walked in the street at night. I didn't feel scared before then. I just wanted to go back home after that.

The death of Kelso Cochrane

In 1959 trouble flared up again in Notting Hill. In May of that year a West Indian carpenter called Kelso Cochrane was murdered by a gang of six white youths as he was walking home in a Notting Hill street. Although there were witnesses to this attack, the murderers were never found and many people in the community felt increasingly bitter that the culprits were never caught. Although it was black people who suffered as a result of these racist attacks, some people used the 'disturbances' of 1958 and 1959 as an excuse to argue for stricter immigration controls.

After several years of debate and controversy the Commonwealth Immigrants Bill of 1961 was passed, creating a voucher system with restricted entry from the West Indies and other countries of the New Commonwealth. Thus the 'open door' policy was abandoned and the flow of West Indians to Britain declined rapidly after the bill became law in 1962.

TESTIMONY

'At that time, when we were in Leicester, there weren't many coloured people around . . . except for the men. People had seen men but they never see a woman . . . never see a black woman. I feel like when you take a fish out of the sea and put it on the sand . . . you can just imagine!'

'I stopped thinking about Britain as the mother country in the first year, in the first months . . . the sense of belonging is not there.'

'I had a feeling that I was a visitor and, like my children feel that they belong here this is their country, I felt that I had to tread softly because I was a visitor.'

'I couldn't stand the smell of the buses and the cars. It was a completely different smell. I just couldn't understand ... well habits y'know, just funny little habits like putting the bread — no paper on it — underneath the pram....'

'I've got a lot of positive things out of England ... my outlook is much wider. I've come up against prejudices but I've also met some wonderful people ... not just black people. There are white people I am close to and it's not just on the surface.'

'There was a certain amount of culture shock. There was no fruit: there were only apples and oranges and if you wanted anything more exotic you rushed to buy one ... something that would cost the earth.... I suppose we were still recovering from the war ... life was still fairly drab for a lot of people.'

'It was really cold, but I didn't have to go out unless it was necessary ... I was indoors most of the time. It wouldn't have been the same back in Trinidad ... I mean people have their windows open, their doors open ... and they're out. Yes, that was something I found difficult to adjust to; having to be sort of ... cooped in, yes that was pretty hard....'

'I was amazed that people actually didn't know anything about the West Indies and we knew all about them. First you feel angry and then I think it's a survival thing and you start to feel sorry for them ... I remember once on the street someone asked me where I had put my tail and the person was serious and I looked at him and I said "the same place where you keep yours".'

DEVELOPMENTS

1 One of the women speaks about 'culture shock' in relation to the different kinds of food that were available in her home island and in England. What do you think she means by 'culture shock'? In what other areas of her life might it have been felt? It might help if you thought about whether you have ever experienced anything like 'culture shock'.

2 The following is taken from the handbook issued by the government of Barbados to everyone who migrated from there to Britain in the 1950s:

> You will find that people in the United Kingdom are less inclined to join you in conversation than your own people in Barbados. This is not meant to be a slight to you but is merely one of the characteristics of the English people. The British are said to be hard to get to know. They like to get things done with the least effort and consider that too much talking is a waste of time. This does not mean that they are unfriendly. If you need help, ask for it and you will find that it is readily given.
>
> You should try to learn quickly how English people do things. These are different from some of your own but not so different that you will not learn them quickly. If you adapt yourself to their way of living you should soon be accepted as one of them, but it is up to you. Remember the old saying 'When in Rome do as Rome does'....
> (Egginton, 1957, p. 161)

What assumptions does this piece make about

(a) English people?
(b) the way in which English people will relate to newcomers?
(c) the way in which the 'newcomers' ought to relate to the English?

3 As we have seen in the testimony and notes, the women who arrived from the Caribbean knew a great deal about the English. However, the English knew little about them. Discuss in what areas of social life this understanding or lack of it would be most apparent.

Describe a meeting between an English person and a West Indian person in which this lack of understanding is shown.

9 Bringing up Children

BACKGROUND NOTES

During the 1950s, although there was a small but regular inflow of children from the West Indies coming to join their parents in Britain, the vast majority were left behind in the first stage of the migration process. However, there was a high proportion of young West Indian children in Britain, many of whom were born here. We have already looked at the problems faced by women with regard to childcare when their children were very small (see section 6, p. 40-1). Many of the worries and anxieties faced by the women in these early days continued as their children entered school and began to come into contact with greater numbers of other children.

Schools

By the early fifties some British schools in large cities already had children representing many different cultures among their pupils. These included the children of post-war European immigrants (e.g. Poles, Italians). By the time children of West Indian origin began to enter the school system, although individual efforts were made to stimulate interest or give help, there was little or no guidance from the government or local education authorities on the needs, the background, or the discrimination they might have to face as they entered schools. It was expected, however, that they would *assimilate* and adopt the values, the behaviour, and the aspirations of their 'host country'.

Many of the women who were interviewed found that their young children were facing hostility and discrimination when they began attending primary school. They complained that teachers had low expectations of their children. For some, it became clear that the problems of discrimination and expressions of racial prejudice in the wider society must inevitably affect the relationships which can be formed in the classroom between pupils of different racial origins and between teachers and pupils. According to an enquiry by *The Times* newspaper of schools in the Midlands (published on 4 November 1963) friendship between children of different ethnic backgrounds did not continue outside the school gates. Many children faced racist name-calling.

The women involved in the Motherland Project responded in varying ways to this situation. Some went into school to complain — others had decided it was best to say nothing. Whatever their response — and even when it was received sympathetically — little was done to improve the situation as no policy had been laid down about how to deal with racial discrimination in schools.

Moreover, the low status of black children in schools in the late 1950s and early 1960s was reinforced by school textbooks and readers. These rarely showed black people at all, but if they did they were portrayed as 'primitive' people living in 'African jungles'. Early readers showed only white children and white adults playing all the dominant and attractive roles.

Many of the women who had left older children in the West Indies faced a different set of problems when families were reunited in Britain. Children who had been left in the care of a grandmother were now adolescents. Some had been separated from their parents for as long as eight years and found it a great strain adjusting to the different requirements at home and at school. Many parents

found, therefore, that they had to reassert their authority over their children when they arrived in Britain, particularly so since English children were generally allowed more scope. Parents also felt that their own views on education and discipline were being challenged by the British school system.

In addition some West Indian parents were becoming increasingly concerned at the number of their children who were being wrongly placed in remedial classes and educationally subnormal (ESN) schools. Because they were unable to appreciate the needs of the West Indian child newly-arrived in Britain, some schools simply categorized these children as slow learners. (This concern was expressed a decade later in the work of Bernard Coard. In 1971 he published what was to prove an important study: *How the West Indian Child is Made Educationally Subnormal in the British School System*. This was widely read by parents, teachers and policy makers and became a rallying point for action among the black community.)

The generation gap

Much has been written about the gap between the first generation of West Indian migrants to Britain and their sons and daughters born in the UK (see, for example, Sue Sharpe, 1976, Chapter 8). Some reports indicate that members of the second generation raised in England inevitably challenge their parents' traditional beliefs. They show how they are torn between the world of their parents and that of their own generation. It is true that young West Indians may have very different attitudes than their parents to English whites, to the police and to employment. It is not only that they are British born, but that their experience of racial discrimination differs from that of their parents who were in the West Indies during their formative years. Growing up in England and sharing classrooms with English children provides them with a different set of expectations.

On the other hand, there are clear lines of continuity between the two generations. Nancy Foner's study of Jamaican migrants to London showed that shared membership of the family, particularly with mothers and children, and a shared sense of being black created strong ties between the two generations. The work of the Motherland Project confirms this bond. Many mothers and daughters shared a pride in their background and in their common struggle as black women. This pride made their understanding of one another stronger in spite of their differences.

Sam King, who arrived on the *Empire Windrush* in 1948, predicted what these differences might be. Interviewed nearly twenty years ago, about the generation gap, he stated: 'I think the only difference between the people on the Windrush and our children is this: we came asking for our rights; they are going to demand them' (Rose, 1969, p. 440).

TESTIMONY

'I taught them not to feel that just because they were born in London they are more special than the person who comes up from the West Indies because in the long run they are going to be treated just the same. Although they may feel very equal with their peers at school they just have to, as unfair as it seems, they have to do that little bit extra from the day when they leave school and get a job.'

'The way I did it is to give my children the best education they can have. I think it's very important; education is a lifelong thing, once you've got it no one can take it away from you.'

'We tried as much as possible to prepare our kids from the time they were toddlers. We tried not to fight their battles for them but to prepare them for coming up against prejudice. We try as much as possible to give them some values. The battles we had to fight in coming to London, if we didn't have the background, the values grounded in us we would not have been able to stand up to a lot of things. So we would try to make them feel proud of being black and teaching them as much as we could about their background.'

'Claudette was the only black child there. So much so that before she went to school the whole school was briefed about this child coming from a different country y'know. She didn't complain ... but when she was nineteen, I found out that this teacher told her that because she's from Trinidad she should be good so that she would be an example to others. And that was a great weight for her.'

58

'My children who were born here know they are Jamaican citizens. They eat Jamaican food, they are Jamaican people — their whole culture, their background is Jamaican. That is something they live with quite comfortably.'

'I said to my children and other young people, "Seek the Lord while you're young for that's the only way to survive in England. Youth is the best time to serve the Lord. If you have him as a young person, then you'll have protection for the rest of your life".'

'I bring my child up just as how I would bring her up in the West Indies. I tell her how my mum grow me. I have to tell her the ways of the people over here are different. You have to be very careful how you move amongst these people....'

'When Diane was about eight or nine there was a little boy living at the end of the street and he used to come for her to go to the Saturday matinee. They used to go every Saturday so they became very friendly. So I always have parties for the children, so I tell Diane to invite him. And Diane said he said to her that his mum say he musn't go into brown people's houses because they have worms. And Diane never spoke to him again....'

DEVELOPMENTS

1 You are one of the women who came over in the 1950s. Your children have been born here and are now young adults. What advice would you give to your daughter in the light of your own experiences?

You might want to advise them in some of the following areas: education, religion, family life, getting a job, relationships within the community.

2 Look at the description, by her mother, of Claudette's experience of being the only black child in the school. This experience was described as 'a great weight for her'. If you were Claudette's mother, and you found out about her situation at school at the time, what would you do about it?

Imagine that Claudette is now an adult and twenty-five years after the experience described in the testimony, she has her own child at school. What kinds of problems might this child face? Would they be the same as Claudette's own problems at school? How might they differ?

3 In the background notes we discussed how the low status of black children in British schools was reinforced by the content and perspective of the textbooks and readers used throughout the 1950s and 1960s.

Look at some of the books you yourself use in school. How is Britain portrayed in these? As a white society? As a multicultural society?

If black people are presented, how are they portrayed? If Caribbean or African countries are described, how are they represented?

10 On Women

BACKGROUND NOTES

When the *Empire Windrush* arrived in Britain in June 1948 there was one woman on board. In spite of the strict ruling that this was to be an all-male migration, there was one female stowaway on the ship — a woman of twenty-five. She introduced herself as Averill Wauchope, a Kingston dressmaker, and was so well liked by the cabin passengers that they raised £50 to help pay her fare and £4 for her immediate needs on arrival in England.

Averill Wauchope may have been the only woman to take part in the famous *Windrush* journey, but by 1953 women began arriving from the West Indies in equal numbers to men. By the mid-1950s thousands of women had left their homes in the Caribbean in the hope that life in Britain would be better for their families and for themselves. Since they were often forced to assume responsibility for housework and childcare their adjustment to life in Britain differed from that of the men. In the workforce, as in the family, women fared differently from men. As we have already seen (section 5) job opportunities were fewer and wages were lower. It was their role as women that shaped the opportunities and experiences available to West Indian female migrants: within the family, at their place of work, and throughout the community.

Hidden from history

Much of the history we read about has, until recently, ignored women's lives altogether. This is usually attributed to the fact that, largely written by white male historians, there has been a failure to ask the questions that might have given us information about the female contribution and the female point of view. According to the feminist historian Gerda Lerner: 'It is necessary to recognize that there is a female aspect to all history, that women were there and that their special contributions to the building and shaping of society were different to those of men' (Lerner, 1973, p. xix).

Similarly, most studies of migration have been written about men. These studies have assumed that women's experience was either identical to men's or not important enough to mention. Our concern with the female aspect of migration throughout the Motherland Project has been an attempt to give the experience of women separate and serious attention.

Women and the community

The enduring and valuable contribution that many West Indian women made to the black community in Britain is often undervalued. As the 'Race Today Women' wrote: 'In one way or another the existence and vibrancy of the black community today is traceable to the social activities of these black women who arrived first' (Race Today Women, 1975, p. 110).

These early women were responsible for the formation of clubs and organizations that gave a sense of identity to the scattered community. (Many of these groups led to the formation of more political organizations in later years like CARD — Campaign Against Racial Discrimination.) The Church often played an important part in the welfare of the community. Women not only formed the majority of the congregation but organized most of the social activities.

Women also took an active role in the creation of self-help saving schemes known as 'pardners'. Each member contributed a regular sum of money every week and when one needed to spend a large sum of money she drew out a lump sum from the kitty.

In Britain, West Indian women supported one another as they always had done in the Caribbean. According to Joyce Justus, in her study of women's role in West Indian society, this support network was strengthened by the sharing of work and by childminding:

> Women are socialized to be resourceful. Each succeeding generation learns from the preceding what it takes to survive in an environment often unfavourable to women. Women turn to other women for advice and counsel.
> (Justus, 1981, p. 447)

These strong female support networks had to change and adapt with migration and new ways of coping had to be found. This was certainly the case for the majority of the women who took part in the Motherland Project. Many of them were forced to find new survival strategies. Women befriended each other, listened to one another and offered help. Many tell of arrangements made with other women to share childcare — fetching each other's children from school, cooking meals for one another — while working different shifts. In the West Indies the sharing of childcare was usually done within the extended family. In Britain, these networks were revitalised by these strong, active and resourceful women.

Race, sex and class

When we look at the experience of West Indian women who migrated to Britain in the 1950s, it is very clear that they inherited the injustices suffered by all women in Britain at that time. Problems surrounding childbearing, women's health, female participation in the labour force, sexual harassment all applied to them. However, there are factors which distinguish the black woman's struggle. She has needed to have greater self-reliance in order for her and her children to survive in a racist society.

Black women have not only been discriminated against because they are women, but because they are black. The majority of female migrant workers during the 1950s became members of the British working-class. They thus had to endure what has been referred to as the triple oppression of race, sex and class: West Indian women *as a group* have, in other words, had to resist racism, sexism and class domination.

The relation between these three influences has been the focus of much recent discussion (see Suggested Reading). This debate may eventually lead to a significant alliance between those groups concerned with fighting discrimination on the grounds of race, sex, and class in our society.

TESTIMONY

'Most of us are not aware that our experience is special because most black women have such difficult lives. We're so busy making arrangements, life is just one big arrangement ... we're arranging somewhere for the children to be, arranging finding somewhere to live, somewhere to work, we're planning and plotting all the time....'

'As a West Indian woman in this country I feel isolated and unwanted. I don't know how men feel, but that's what it means to me.... The feeling doesn't get any worse it's just there. You know you're not wanted and you just act accordingly, keep yourself to yourself.'

'I don't depend on anyone now. I just try to bring the children up on my own. My mother came here without knowing where she was going or anything and she survived seventeen years of it on her own.'

'Life was much harder for women than it was for men.... I used to have to take the two children to the childminder and go to work in the factory — I had to catch the bus at half-past five.... I come back and use the coal fire. They rent you a room but you can't do anything ... sometimes you had to hide the iron.... You think it is a little hardness we suffer in this country?'

'It's very, very difficult to make anything of yourself here. There's always a barrier. You've got to be very strong ... it's the only way.'

'I think in every race it's always the women who holds things together. The woman does everything. She plans, she decides when they should buy a house, she decides the school the kids should go to, and she has retained all her West Indianness.'

'When you think of it we didn't know the systems; we didn't know about day nurseries. We had babies and we didn't know what we were going to do with them. Really what do you do with a baby when you live in this miserable room in a damp house and you don't know anybody ... and in a really racist society we made friends with white people and gradually learned how the system worked.'

'I think most of the women who came over are really strong. Most of them came on their own, some came before husbands or fiancés came to join them. I think they were really wonderful. They came here, they coped and they are still coping.'

DEVELOPMENTS

1   The women who were interviewed had been discriminated against as migrants. They were also, however, discriminated against because they were women. Sexism as well as racism was an important influence shaping their lives.

What forms did this sex discrimination take?

In what areas of their social, family and working lives did it operate?

2   We have looked at several aspects of the women's lives in Britain: housing, earning a living, childcare, relationships with men, responses to the new community and bringing up children. These are presented in sequence. For many of the women, however, these aspects were experienced all at once. As a result there was a build-up of problems, each one worsening the effect of the others.

Discuss the different kinds of problems that one woman might have had to cope with in a single day.

Write a short story, highlighting the way in which the build-up of these problems has an impact on one woman's life.

3   The debate about race, sex and class is a complicated one. Valerie Amos and Pratibha Parmar (1981) explore many of the issues in their chapter, 'Resistances and Responses: the experience of black girls in Britain,' (see Suggested Reading). Find this book in your school or local library and consider the arguments carefully.

4   In section 1, one of the women was reported to have said: 'West Indians never go anywhere for good'. However, for a variety of reasons the twenty-three women that we interviewed had all chosen or been constrained to stay. Imagine one person's life as you recall the testimony included in the preceding sections. Choosing your own form (poem, diary account, letter or story) write about your reasons for staying.

Part Two
THE PLAY MOTHERLAND

INTRODUCTION

The Motherland Project based at Vauxhall Manor School in south London grew out of a tradition of exploring social and historical issues through drama. The issues that many pupils chose to explore were often directly related to their experiences of being female and black.

Concern with these issues extended beyond the classroom to intensive production work that involved pupils of all ages in collaborative research and experiment. *Slave Girl* (performed at the Oval House Theatre, 1979) was about the effects of slavery on women in nineteenth-century America; *Wicked Women* (performed at the Oval House and Cottesloe Theatre, 1980) looked at the persecution of women as witches in medieval Europe. Personal testimony — people's own accounts of their own experiences — has always had an important part to play in this kind of drama work.

The making of Motherland

Motherland, the third play in the series, is based upon the personal testimony of twenty-three women in the local community who came to Britain from the West Indies in the 1950s. Marcia Smith, a former pupil involved in the previous projects, began by interviewing her own mother and members of her own family. Eventually twenty-three women shared their life stories with us; most of them were the mothers of the girls involved in the play. These accounts, gathered through interview, were supplemented by extensive research into the social history of the period (see Part One). It was through a study of the primary sources — the genuine documents and materials of the time — that the company was able to discover a way of framing the women's accounts of their own experiences.

The play was produced and devised by a multiracial cast of young women, ranging from age 11–19. The company met three times a week for a year. They began by reading transcripts of the interviews and listening to the tapes. These fed directly into the play rehearsals. They worked thematically choosing a particular aspect of the women's experiences to focus on. The notion of experiment underlies all of the work.

The group worked in many different ways: as a whole group with the teacher playing a role; in smaller groups through improvisation; and individually, trying to re-create personal experiences and then writing about them. The company had made the decision early on that each member should have the opportunity of exploring a variety of roles, including both black and white women. Ideas were shared about the tapes as the girls used drama to reflect upon their own interpretation of the women's voices. They worked through mime and movement, wrote verse and told stories. Ritual had a great part to play and song, too, became a powerful element. Excited by a particular aspect of the drama work, girls would come back with new ideas — lyrics sometimes scribbled on crumpled pieces of paper and melodies recorded on tapes. These all became a part of *Motherland*.

At the heart of the project were the twenty-three women. The company wanted to meet with them as often as possible. Through a series of open rehearsals the group shared their interpretation of the women's life stories. At these meetings the women were visibly moved by what they saw, made suggestions, shared anecdotes and songs and pointed out aspects of the play that were inaccurate. One of the daughters, who was a member of the company, summed up what these rehearsals had meant to her: 'When you have to say the testimony that the women have said, when you have to sit there, when you think about it, to say it out, you're not just learning it, you're understanding it. You begin to understand what your parents always told you.'

The performances

Motherland was first performed at the Oval House Theatre in south London on 9 July 1982, and had nine live performances. The video*, upon which the following script is largely based, was recorded at ILEA Television Centre, Battersea from 14–17 March 1983. Although the video was made eight months after the stage production, the company continued to work in the same collaborative way while adapting their stage play for television. Twenty of the original cast of twenty-six took a fresh look at the play — refining and redefining its form and content.

The following text focusses on the period between the coronation of Queen Elizabeth II in 1953 and the first Notting Hill 'riots' of 1958. Each scene explores a different theme. In the main, the development of the play follows the sequence of notes given in Part One, where the main themes of the play have already been outlined.

---

*The video is available for sale or hire: within ILEA from, ILEA Television Centre, Thackeray Road, London SW8; and outside ILEA from Central Film Library, Chalfont St. Giles, Gerrards Cross, Bucks.

A note on the text

The text of *Motherland* combines aspects of the play that were written as script and scenes that were completely improvised and later transcribed from recordings of the performance*. Those parts of the play which were set down as script include the women's testimony, which is taken word for word from the interviews and introduces each scene. Poems and songs that were written by individual members of the company were also incorporated into the final script. Other scenes, although they were finalized and set, were improvised throughout the run of the play and so varied slightly from one performance to another (an example of this is scene 7 — the 'kitchen scene').

Some of the play is written and improvised in what is variously referred to as 'creole', 'patois', or 'dialect'. This is spoken by the vast majority of West Indians in the Caribbean and has a grammar and sound system all of its own. There is a great variety among individuals speaking 'patois' and also differences between the islands. In Britain, more variations occurred as people from different islands mixed with each other and became influenced by local English dialects. The company — even those members who did not have a West Indian background themselves — enjoyed experimenting with West Indian 'dialect' in both the improvised and written parts of the play. The text of *Motherland* uses a wide range of language styles.

The following definitions of words used in *Motherland* may help some of you to follow certain scenes in the play more closely:

a	is, be, am, are; it is, there are; to, of, in, at
cyan	can't
dem	they, them
fe	for, to
gawn	gone
gwine	going to
haffe	have to, need to
lick	hit
likkle	little
mah	mother
nyam	eat, devour
pickney	child, children
teck, tek	take
seh	that
soh	so
unnah (also *unna, oono, unno*)	plural form of you

*The working script of *Motherland* was published in *Ambit 91*, (1982), *Caribbean Special Issue*, 17 Priory Gardens, London N6.

MOTHERLAND

Devised by the Motherland Company, Vauxhall Manor School
Coordinated by Elyse Dodgson
Interviews by Marcia Smith
Songs by:
Marcia Arboine
Sharon Bell
Louisa Eyo
Sylvia Obi
Beverley Russell
Sandra Saunders
Marcia Smith

Motherland was first performed at the Oval House Theatre, Kennington, London, on 9 July 1982 with the following cast:
Marcia Arboine, Sharon Bell, Cheryl Blair, Samantha Ellis, Louisa Eyo, Sharon Gordon, Angela Gayle, Justine Hankins, Simone Kilshaw, Juliette Lindsay, Angela Masters, Diane Masters, Beverley McLean, Joy Morris, Sylvia Obi, Deborah Olver, Jackie Ramsay, Beverley Russell, Sandra Saunders, Christine Savva, Deborah Shorey, Sharon Shorey, Marcia Smith, Tina Smith, Emelia Thompson, Glenis Williamson

The video based on the stage play was recorded from 14—17 March 1983 at ILEA Television Centre, Battersea, London, with the following cast:
Marcia Arboine, Cheryl Blair, Samantha Ellis, Louisa Eyo, Angela Gayle, Justine Hankins, Simone Kilshaw, Angela Masters, Diane Masters, Joy Morris, Sylvia Obi, Beverley Russell, Sandra Saunders, Christine Savva, Deborah Shorey, Sharon Shorey, Marcia Smith, Tina Smith, Emelia Thompson, Glenis Williamson

Costumes by Alison Seal
Design and artwork by Pete Jones
Choreography by Rose Bellot
Music coordination by Rob Cox
Directed by Elyse Dodgson

MOTHERLAND

Scene 1

(MARCIA's *mother is seated at kitchen table drinking tea.* MARCIA, *aged nineteen, carrying briefcase and tape recorder enters.*)

MARCIA   Hi, Mum.
MOTHER   Hello, Marcia. Oh I'm so tired.
MARCIA   You going to work tonight?
MOTHER   Yes, late night again.
MARCIA   Listen Mum. I've got a favour to ask of you.
MOTHER   What now, money?
MARCIA   Another interview.
MOTHER   Look Marcia, I gave you one of those interviews, what, two, three days ago.
MARCIA   I know Mum, but you can't cram your life into one interview. This won't take long, just ten minutes.
MOTHER   Look I don't want to cram my whole life into one interview. I already told you the general story. I come over in the fifties like a lot of other people. There've been good times and bad times.
MARCIA   That's right Mum, you told me the general story but I want to know more details about your experiences over here.
MOTHER   Look you want to know more details. A lot of other people want to know more detail; they gonna take it from this play you're going to make.
MARCIA   Look Mum, a lot of good can come from it as well.
MOTHER   Good like what?
MARCIA   Well maybe our generation, my generation, can learn from your experiences. Please Mum, do it for me.
MOTHER   (*she sighs*) So where you want me to carry on from then?
MARCIA   Right, well last time we were talking about you growing up in the West Indies. What I'd like to know is more about how you felt about England then. (*She puts the tape recorder on and places it in front of her* MOTHER.)
MOTHER   Well, we used to sing songs about England. You know like (*she sings*) 'Rule Britannia, Britannia rule the wave' and we used to chant 'Red, white and blue, what does it mean to you? Shout it aloud, Britain's awake. These are the chains that nothing can break.' Those are the songs we grew up with and we had to dress up in blue skirt and white blouse when they having these coronations, or when they crowning Queen Elizabeth and King George. Yes we felt very much involved and we had to sing (*she sings*) 'There'll always be an England and England shall be free, if England mean so much to you as England mean to me.'

MARCIA   Did you know any people from England then?
MOTHER   Well the only people we knew were the preacher men they used to send over and all these little ladies they call 'band of mercy' ladies who used to come and talk about 'Don't kill the birds, the little birds that fly among the trees', and the impression they give us is like everyone over there is like that, so nice and sweet that in England it must be fantastic.

(*Lights fade on* MARICA *and her* MOTHER. *Lights up on the entire company slowly doing jobs they would have been doing in the West Indies. Some are washing, some are looking after children, some are working in the fields. Each girl is completely absorbed in a job — there is only occasional talk.*)

Scene 2
The West Indies, 1953

SYLVIA   Elvira, bring the washing ...
SANDRA   How's your son love? ...
LOUISA   He's alright ...

(*The women continue absorbed in their jobs until they are interrupted by a voice over the loudspeaker. They slowly stop what they are doing and listen.*)

ANNOUNCER   (*A BBC recording of the Queen's coronation*) 'The Queen is still sitting in King Edward's chair. The princes and princesses, the peers and peeresses prepare to put on their coronets and caps.... The archbishop assisted by other bishops comes forward. The Dean of Westminster brings the crown. The archbishop takes it from the crimson cushion, he raises it high in the sight of the people and reverently places it on the Queen's head. Her Majesty Queen Elizabeth the Second is crowned!'

ALL   (*singing — backed by the sound of a single steel drum*)
   England, sweet England
   Is dere we gwine live
   The air is so different
   But our labour we a give
   Even though we know
   (Even though we know)
   The difference is big
   Sweet England, we comin to live

(*The women hum, continue their jobs as individuals speak.*)

WOMAN 1   I'm going to England because my mother sent for me. I'm staying five years.
WOMAN 2   I'm going to England because I hear that other people are doing good. I'm going to stay about three years.
WOMAN 3   I'm going to England because there's no employment here. I'm staying two years.
WOMAN 4   I'm going to England because my fiancé is there. I'm staying five years.
WOMAN 5   I'm going to England to do nursing training. I'm staying three years.
WOMAN 6   I'm going to England because it is my mother country.
WOMAN 7   I'm going to England to make money. I'm staying one year.

WOMAN 8   I'm going to England to join my husband. I'm staying four years.
WOMAN 9   I'm going to England because they said they needed me; I'm not sure how long I am staying.
WOMAN 10   I'm going to England to ensure a better future for my children. I'm staying for as long as it takes.
SANDRA AND LOUISA   *(sing)*
    Jamaica, Trinidad and Grenada, Barbados...
    We leave you behind
    Every little thing
    Gwine be different, we will find
ALL   Even though we know
    (Even though we know)
    The difference is big
    Sweet England, we're coming to live
(Still finishing off their jobs.)
    England, sweet England
    Is dere we gwine live
    The air is so different
    But our labour we a give
    Even though we know
    (Even though we know)
    The difference is big
    Sweet England, we're coming to live

Scene 3

(Another interviewee is speaking into the tape recorder.)
INTERVIEWEE   Yes, it was the first time I'd left the country. I did go to Barbados and the West Indian islands, but it was the first time I'd left home, friends and family. They had a big party the night we left and loads of friends and relatives came to wave us goodbye. I promised to come back in five years. It was a very emotional time. I looked at everybody waving at the harbour and went into the cabin and burst into tears, came back and waved so they didn't know. But I felt that lost, you know, just leaving — even though I was coming to meet my husband. I wasn't lookin forward to coming to England. I would have been quite happy to stay in Trinidad. I just came because he was here.
(Lights up on DEBORAH busily packing her suitcase. Her daughter, SHARON, is helping her.)
SHARON   Mum, why you packing so early?
DEBORAH   Look you know I like to have all my tings ready, when I'm ready to go. Now let me see... look now pass me them shoes over there.
SHARON   Which ones?
DEBORAH   You just act so blasted stupid sometimes. Look you know I only wear the plain ones; now pick them up and bring them over here.
SHARON   Mum, Judy's mum had a party the night before she went to England.

DEBORAH   And I'll have a party before I'm ready to go, but I'm not ready to go. Look, you want some sweets?

SHARON   Sweeties? Now?

DEBORAH   *(taking some money out of her handbag)* Look you go and buy some sweets for yourself. But you be careful how you cross that road *(she takes Sharon's hand)* because you know those boys down by that corner, they're like madmen ...

SHARON   Mum you're squeezing my hand. ... You will be here when I get back?

DEBORAH   Look girl, go and buy your sweets! *(SHARON runs off and DEBORAH looks longingly after her. GRANDMOTHER enters.)*

GRANDMOTHER   Deborah! Deborah! Didn't you hear me calling you.

DEBORAH   I was doing some tings over here. *(She hands her a straw bag.)* I was looking for this bag everywhere this morning you know.

GRANDMOTHER   You leave that on the bed last night.

DEBORAH   I had a feeling I left it there. Anyway, I have all my tings ready here and I'm ready to go. ... Look don't start crying now because you are going to make me cry too cause you know how emotional I am already.

GRANDMOTHER   You know I can't help it.

DEBORAH   You promise to look after Sharon for mi.

GRANDMOTHER   Of course I will. ... Look if you don't like it you can always come back you know.

DEBORAH   I'm coming back anyway. I'm not going to England for good.

GRANDMOTHER   Well, the only advice I have to give to you: keep you principles up and ... I love you.

(They embrace. DEBORAH continues to pack. ANGELA enters.)

ANGELA   You ready to go? You don't have to go you know you can always stay.

DEBORAH   Look, I hope you haven't come over here to change my mind, because I'm ready to go.

ANGELA   I want to give you this. *(She hands her a photograph.)*

DEBORAH   I can't take that.

ANGELA   Please I want you to take it.

DEBORAH   Do you remember when we took this picture?

ANGELA   It was down by the river.

DEBORAH   We got licks for it too! You promise to write to mi. I'll write to you.

ANGELA   Take care of yourself you hear. I'll miss you you know. *(They embrace.)* Goodbye. *(ANGELA moves down right and EMELIA enters.)*

EMELIA   Deborah. *(She enters carrying a cardigan. DEBORAH examines it.)*

DEBORAH   It's lovely you know and it fit me just right. Anyway I'll take it off and put it in the suitcase.

EMELIA   I want you to have the best cardigan in England.

DEBORAH   You is a lovely women. Come kiss mi. *(They embrace.)*

EMELIA   Don't get seasick. *(She moves down left, slightly above GRANDMOTHER. CHERYL enters.)*

CHERYL   Deborah, you all ready? You've got your suitcase packed to the brim. ... I just wanted to say goodbye. Look just take this then. You don't have to thank me cause it's just brass. *(She puts a ring on her finger.)* Take care of yourself you hear and write to me.

(*They embrace.*) Well, take care then.

DEBORAH   (*Takes CHERYL's hand.*) Look this isn't anything final you know. I'm going to England for what two or three years, not for good. West Indians never go anywhere for good because we live in these islands and the economic situation is so bad that we're used to going away. We just come back, I will come back.

(*DEBORAH shuts the suitcase and starts to pick up her bags as Sharon enters.*)

SHARON   Mum. (*She realizes that her mother is leaving.*)

DEBORAH   I'm sorry Sharon . . . but you will kiss your mother goodbye?

(*Deborah moves slightly towards SHARON, but SHARON freezes. The others surround SHARON, holding and supporting her. DEBORAH speaks the following verse to SHARON, while SHARON and the others sing to DEBORAH 'Before you go away'.*)

DEBORAH   My last night at home
I see my likkle girl a cry
So I hold her in my hand
An I start to dry her eye

I say,
Don't cry my baby
I'll be back some day
I don't goin' forever
I not goin' to stay

She turn an look at me
Her eye holdin' a tear
She cried mama I love you
An I cry because I scared

So I teck her on my lap
And through me I feel she fear
Slowly I draw her to me
And whisper in my daughter's ear

Don't cry my baby
I'll be back some day
I don't goin' forever
I not goin' to stay
You is my only daughter

Song *Before you go away*
This first verse is sung quietly while DEBORAH *speaks the above to* SHARON.

Before you go away, into the dark dull day
Remember where you're going, remember where you're going to stay
Remember you are black and I hope that you'll be coming back
Remember you are mine, and girl to me you're fine
Before you go, I want you to know
Before you go, I want you to know
Before you go, I want you to know,

>   That there is someone, someone who loves you so
>
> *This second verse is sung in full voice by SHARON and others to DEBORAH.*
>   When you reach the land, that you don't understand
>   Behave yourself for me, and don't you bring down the family
>   Remember you are black, and I hope that you'll be coming back
>   Remember you are mine, and girl to me you're fine
>   Before you go, I want you to know
>   Before you go, I want you to know
>   Before you go, I want you to know
>   That there is someone, someone who loves you so

Scene 4

INTERVIEWEE   1953. I leave the 22nd of September and I reach on the 5th October. I come on a ship named *Monasty*, a German boat — only twelve passengers on that boat. The journey was quite nice you know, but me wasn't well. After the ship pull out I didn't even know me was so far from the wharf until somebody say look down, and when me look down me was far away and it was moving off gradually. Me see the water and everything.

(There is a sound of ships' horns and seagulls as six of the women face each other, waving goodbye, and shouting out last minute words of advice 'Don't forget to write', 'Don't forget me', 'Don't get seasick'. In the video version, newspaper advertisements from the Daily Gleaner *of 1955 are shown on the screen, describing some of the ships that are carrying passengers to England. The image of the women on the ship recedes into the distance as one woman continues to wave goodbye.)*

Scene 5
England 1953–8

INTERVIEWEE   It was a cold cold November day. People were so cold. I wanted to turn around and go back; it had all been a horrible mistake. I don't want to do nursing, I don't want to be here. I didn't realize it would have been that cold and it was misty. Now I can look back and say it was misty; at the time it was dense fog. One of the things that shocked me was looking around and seeing English people doing manual work. It seemed so depressing, the picture that I had built up in my mind. It wasn't that I thought it was the golden land but the streets, the space, the accent, the strange accent.... There were curious onlookers standing around looking; anxious black people and curious white people....

(BEVERLEY arrives on stage with her suitcase during the end of this speech. She is lost and bewildered. She is also pregnant.)

BEVERLEY   I feel utterly despairing, a feeling of total confusion, I've arrived. I've left home and I've arrived here.

(The entire company enters greeting each other, trailing belongings, wandering about lost and alone as the sounds of Waterloo station are heard in the background.)
NEWSPAPER VENDOR   Get your *Daily Mail* here!
(The company freeze in tableau as a single scene is presented.)
WOMAN   Excuse me, can you show me the way to Birmingham?
CLEANER   Hmmm. Why don't you take a taxi?
WOMAN   Can you show me where me can get a taxi?
CLEANER   Why don't you go to the information desk?
(The company come alive again and continue to have encounters until:)
NEWSPAPER VENDOR   Get your *Daily Mail* here.
WOMAN 2   Tina is that you? *(Her child is looking lost, sitting on her suitcase. She grabs her.)* Let me see you child, turn round let me see you ...
TINA   Mum, I don't think I'm gonna like it here.
WOMAN 2   You'll like it when I show you Big Ben. *(She takes her off. The company continue to create chaos. WOMAN 3 thinks she has spotted someone and chases her to the far end of the stage.)*
WOMAN 3   Wait! ... Angela ... Angela ... ANGELA. *(The girl turns to face her.)* I'm sorry. I thought she was Angela. That girl favour Angela — she favour Angela eh?
(The company slowly move off leaving BEVERLEY waiting with three other women.)
BEVERLEY   I never knew it was so cold over here you know.
SHARON   Yes it's really cold.
BEVERLEY   I'm waiting for my husband you see.
SHARON   Oh, I'm waiting for me sister.
BEVERLEY   Oh ...
SHARON   You've got the time?
SAMANTHA   It's ten past six at the moment love.
SHARON   Ten past six and she said she would meet me at 5 o'clock.
SAMANTHA   Maybe she got lost.
SHARON   I don't think so.
SAMANTHA   I'm waiting for my brother you know. His name Arthur. He live in ummm ... I can't even remember.
BEVERLEY   My husband live in Brixton.
SAMANTHA   Nice place?
BEVERLEY   I don't know ... but he work for London Transport.
SAMANTHA   What sort of London Transport?
BEVERLEY   Uhmmm ... I tink it's the buses, yes it's the buses.
SAMANTHA   I wonder where he is, he take his time eh?
(WOMAN enters carrying an overcoat.)
WOMAN   You ladies been waiting here long? You didn't happen to see a tall handsome man go past?
WOMEN   No *(She exits.)*
SHARON   Poor woman, she lost her husband.
SAMANTHA   See Arthur over there. I hope to meet you ladies another time, you hear ... ARTHUR! *(She runs off.)*
BEVERLEY   That's nice ... You know someting.

SHARON   What?
BEVERLEY   My husband's been over here two years...
SHARON   *(She looks at her big belly.)* Two years? *(She smiles.)*
BEVERLEY   He's a very nice man you see.
SHARON   He must be.... I'm sure she give me her address you know. It must be here somewhere. *(She looks through her handbag.)* Yes me have it here. Well it's no use me standing around when I can just get a uhmmm taxi.
BEVERLEY   You sure love?
SHARON   Yes I'm sure.... Look, me hope your husband comes soon. *(Exits.)* Alright? Alright, bye love!
BEVERLEY   Lord I never knew it was so cold over here. I wonder where Cecil is.... Oh look see he a comes... no that's not Cecil. *(She watches a man approaching her and moves away.)* I wonder what this man tink him a go. *(She listens to him.)* What? I'm waiting for me husband. Look why you tell me you got a house for, me want to know about a house? Because me hear about unnah men in England y'know how unnah pick up woman at station and bring to unnah house and murder them. You want to murder me? Just go about your business and leave me alone.
(WOMAN enters again, with coat.)
WOMAN   You still waiting here?
BEVERLEY   Yes I'm waiting for me husband, he hasn't come til now you know.
WOMAN   You must be cold then.
BEVERLEY   Yes I'm really cold.
WOMAN   Well I can't find my husband no way so you can have this coat.
BEVERLEY   You sure love? Come and help me put it on then.... You must give me your address so me can send you back the coat, y'know.
WOMAN   No, I can't find him so you can keep it. I'd like to stop here chatting a bit longer, but when I start I can't stop. I did leave the kids at home you see because I did think I could come here and find this blasted man waiting for me and I just have to look everywhere for him. Well, I can't stop. Bye.
BEVERLEY   Oh this coat's lovely and warm eh? Look at that fool fool man come back again fe bother me. So you come back again?... But it's really cold over here fe true.... So what part of Jamaica you say you're from... St Elizabeth! Well I was born and grown there, yes, man.... You say you have heater and tings.... Oh... you say you can put me up for the night. You will? Oh alright then. I don't usually do this sort of ting you know, cause I'm a married woman... but since you come from St Elizabeth.... You come from Black River? Alright come along then. *(She exits talking to him.)*

Scene 6

INTERVIEWEE   I noticed the grey dull buildings... the houses are like prisons... how wet and dark everywhere is... you would go into a building and you think that it wasn't open but when you go in you see a light. From outside it looked like if the place was shut because you're used to open places... open doors. I couldn't believe it. We encountered lots and lots of problems looking for somewhere to live... the white folks

didn't want to know. Sometimes they just closed the door in your face. Even with the blacks.... Blacks didn't want anybody with children. I was looking for a better reception towards us.... No vacancy ... I wouldn't have left Jamaica if I'd known. I lost days from work looking for a room ... the situation was very bad. I felt very bitter.
(Lights up on women and children walking the streets of England with their belongings. There are a few static figures scattered among them; they are the landladies. A knock is heard and LANDLADY 1 *mimes opening a door.)*

LANDLADY 1   Yes, what do you want?
WOMAN 1   I've been looking for a place to live all day and everybody turn me down. I wonder if you can give me a little room.
LANDLADY 1   I'm sorry I haven't got any rooms. *(Door is shut.)*

[Song '*Searchin*' interrupts the dialogue throughout the following sequence.]
(Lights up on the singers.)
SINGER 1   Searchin, wow I'm searchin
SINGER 2   Tryin to find a place to rest
SINGER 3   Searchin keep on searchin
　　　　　England you put me to your test

(A knock and LANDLADY 2 *opens door.)*
LANDLADY 2   Yes.
WOMAN 2   I see a vacancy sign in your window and I was wondering if you still have a room.
LANDLADY 2   Well, we do have one room.
WOMAN 2   Well I promise you I won't be any trouble and I will pay you in advance.
LANDLADY 2   Well, I'll just go and check with my husband.... *(Pause.)* Excuse me, I'm most terribly sorry, my husband says the room is already gone.
WOMAN 2   But there's a vacancy sign in your window.
LANDLADY 2   He must have forgotten to take it out.
WOMAN 2   Yes, I understand. *(Door is shut.)*
SINGER 1   You're tryin oh so very hard
　　　　　To see how far I'm gonna go
SINGER 2   And when I get there I'm gonna see
SINGER 3   You'll break me up before I know
LANDLADY 3   What do you want?
WOMAN 3   *(accompanied by her child)* We've been walking all day, me and my child and I'm looking for a room.
LANDLADY 3   I'm sorry I've got no rooms to let.
WOMAN 3   But there's a vacancy sign in the window.
LANDLADY 3   It's none of your business what I've got in my window. And besides I don't take no one with children. *(Door is shut.)*
WOMAN 4   *(Knocks on landlady's door.)*
LANDLADY 4   You've been walking all day and your feet hurt. You want a room. Well I'm sorry we don't allow niggers in this house. *(Door is shut.)*
3 SINGERS   I won't stop searchin, wow I'm searchin

    Tryin to find a place to rest
    Searchin keep on searchin
    England you put me to your test

    You think you're gonna chew me up
    That this is just some more black meat
    So listen hear black woman
    Come along and take your back row seat

    I won't stop searchin, wow I'm searchin
    Tryin to find a place to rest
    Searchin keep on searchin
    England you put me to your test
    (Repeat chorus and England you put me to your test, six times)

(A knock and LANDLADY 6 opens the door.)

WOMAN 6   Excuse me madam, I was passing your house and I see the vacancy sign and I was wondering if you still had a room.

LANDLADY 6   Yes, I have a room.

WOMAN 6   Thank the Lord, I've been walking 2000 miles....

LANDLADY 6   *(She interrupts.)* I'll tell you someting. I've got three tenants already — they give me problems.

WOMAN 6   Me no give you no problem you know me promise you that.

LANDLADY 6   Do you have any children?

WOMAN 6   No children at all.

LANDLADY 6   Make sure you're out of my kitchen before I come home. Use my bathroom after I've gone to work. I don't want to see you or hear you when I get to this house. No electric iron or heater unless I give you permission and I charge for it then. No visitors during the week — Sunday only. If you're not back in this house by 10 don't bother to come back.

WOMAN 6   *(She keeps nodding and agreeing.)* I'll remember that.

LANDLADY 6   Thirty shillings in advance, take it or leave it.

WOMAN 6   I'll take it.

LANDLADY 6   Come in.

Scene 7

(Lights up on MISS MATTIE cooking on a small stove. She is stirring and tasting the contents of a dutch pot.)

MISS MATTIE (singing)   We are rolling on
                          We are rollin on
                          Under the tree of life
                          We are rollin on . . .

(She continues humming as MISS MARSHALL arrives from work.)

MISS MARSHALL   Good evening, Miss Mattie.

MISS MATTIE   Oh, hello, Miss Marshall. Is how you be?

MISS MARSHALL   You still 'pon the stove?
MISS MATTIE   Yes, man. Y'know seh me haffe cook fe Wilfred and the two pickney them?
MISS MARSHALL   Y'know Miss Mattie every evening is the same ting. Seh me come in six o'clock and not for nothing would you come off the stove and furthermore you're using both the burners.

(MISS JOYCE *enters.*)

MISS JOYCE   Evening.
MISS MARSHALL   Evening, Miss Joyce. You ever see me dyin' trials?
MISS JOYCE   You still 'pon the burners then?
MISS MATTIE   Miss Joyce, Miss Marshall. Unnah have to sympathize wid me y'know. Unnah no seh me have to cook fe Wilfred and the two pickney them?
MISS JOYCE   Sympathize what? I hope you know that I did put two shilling in that meter this morning, y'know.
MISS MARSHALL   Me see you.
MISS JOYCE   And I hope you never burn it out.
MISS MATTIE   Burn it out? You ever work two shillings to put in that meter. Burn it out!
MISS MARSHALL   What a woman! (*Mutters under her breath, then sees* MISS SMITH, *the landlady.*) Oh hello, Miss Smith.
MISS JOYCE   Good evening, Miss Smith.
MISS SMITH   Good evening Miss Marshall and Miss Joyce. But Miss Mattie, you mean to tell me you still 'pon that stove?
MISS MATTIE   You have to bear with me y'know. Y'know seh me have to cook fe Wilfred and the two pickney them.
MISS SMITH   But Miss Mattie everybody in this house must use that stove. You cannot understand that?
MISS MATTIE   Alright then. Give me half an hour.
MISS SMITH   Anyway Miss Joyce, when you intend to pay your rent?
MISS JOYCE   I was going to pay you rent next week y'know. Anyway, me get a job interview tomorrow, y'know. Me know seh me will get it. Me can feel it in my soul.
MISS SMITH   Like the job before that and the job before that. (MISS MARSHALL *tries to sneak off.*) But Miss Marshall where you think you a go? I want a word with you too. When you intend to pay your rent?
MISS MARSHALL   Ah, Miss Smith. I'm so glad you bring up the subject. Miss Smith, my mother's sick. I had to send her a few pound to help her out. Y'know how it go Miss Smith.
MISS SMITH   So you payin' fe house in Jamaica and you living here?
MISS MARSHALL   Miss Smith, I'll pay you the rent next week. I promise you. Miss Smith, how many times I'm ever back on the rent since you know me? Talk the truth, Miss Smith.
MISS SMITH   You want me to talk the truth?
MISS MATTIE   Well Miss Smith, y'know my husband never back down on the rent.
MISS SMITH   I'll soon come back in here fe unnah. (*She exits.*)
MISS MARSHALL   (*to* MISS MATTIE) And you! I'm gonna put my things down and when I come back I want the burner please! (*She exits.*)
MISS JOYCE   Y'still'pon the stove with your big pot of rice and meat and y'can't tell me seh

you can share out some give us?
MISS MATTIE   Share out some and give unnah? When my Wilfred work and sweat blood fe feed we?
MISS JOYCE   Sweat blood what? With that big pot belly and two fat children them and him sweat blood? Bwoy you craven soh!
(Enter MISS MARSHALL.)
MISS MARSHALL   Excuse me love, let me find me rice. *(She looks in the cupboard.)* Wait a minute. I left a five-pound bag of rice in here this morning and it gone and I want to know who take it. *(She looks at MISS MATTIE.)*
MISS JOYCE   Ah, she take it y'know. *(Pointing at MISS MATTIE.)* And me, this morning, my meat gone!
MISS MARSHALL   *(She tries to make her way to the stove to look in MISS MATTIE's pot.)* Just hold on a minute, Miss Joyce. *(Miss Smith re-enters unnoticed.)*
MISS MATTIE   Look, no bother spit in me food. Lord! Unnah blame me? Say me tek unnah rice and unnah meat when the Lord in heaven knows seh me no take it.
MISS MARSHALL   No bother call the Lord in vain, Miss Mattie!
MISS JOYCE   Y'go to church and you lie. We gwine tell Miss Smith.
MISS SMITH   It was not Miss Mattie who took unnah rice and unnah meat. It was me.
MISS MARSHALL   Why?
MISS SMITH   Well unnah not payin in fe unnah rent, so how am I supposed to live?
MISS JOYCE   But me pay good money for that meat, Miss Smith.
MISS SMITH   So you pay good money for that meat and you cannot pay your rent?
MISS MARSHALL   Anyway, Miss Smith, I've got a complaint to make, Miss Smith. Miss Mattie been cookin' out of me dutch pot all week and she don't even wash it and turn it down. Miss Smith, you can't talk to her?
MISS MATTIE   Miss Smith, y'see what me have fe put up with. Ah! When me come 'pon the boat, Miss Smith, y'know me granny give me that dutch pot.
MISS MARSHALL   Miss Smith, is lie, she lying.
MISS SMITH   Look, stop confusing me soul and let the woman talk.
MISS MATTIE   Miss Smith, when me come 'pon the boat, y'know, the dutch pot drop and dent. Look Miss Smith, a no lie me tell, look see the dent there!
MISS MARSHALL   Miss Smith, it's my dutch pot!
MISS SMITH   It's not your dutch pot. It is Miss Mattie's dutch pot fe true. One of she child bring down your dutch pot and I refuse to bring it back up here.
MISS JOYCE   But what she gwine cook out of?
MISS SMITH   What she gwine cook out of? She ain't got no business cookin' in my kitchen no more 'cause I want both of unnah out of my house before midnight tonight.
MISS MARSHALL   But Miss Smith?
MISS SMITH   Don't bother fe call me name. Me just want both of unnah out of me house. *(She exits.)*
MISS JOYCE   Not even a day notice.
MISS MARSHALL   What we gwine do, Miss Joyce?
MISS JOYCE   Me no know. *(They exit.)*
MISS MATTIE *(singing)*   We are rollin on
 We are rollin on

Under the tree of life
We are rollin on . . .
(She continues to hum as she checks on her dinner.)

Scene 8

INTERVIEWEE   So we go to Nottingham. Couldn't find nowhere. You know where we leave we tings, we tings what we go with? Down at the train station. Somebody tell we to go up the road and this woman leave her room and give us. Then she say she never see a coloured woman before, she see a few coloured men in the war days, but she never see a coloured woman before. And after we living there the woman was quite happy to get we money . . . for she a pubber. All in the summer she go to the pub, but some of the people dem give her a cold shoulder and didn't want to talk to her. Say she have coloured people in her house. So what you tink? Dem start to show her bad face.

(Lights up on pub table where three women are drinking.)
SIMONE   Did I tell you 'bout my son the other day?
DEBORAH   No, go on!
SIMONE   You know I told you he had a new friend at school. Well I told him to bring him home 'cause I like to know who he's mixing with.
DEBORAH   Yeah, that's best.
SIMONE   Well, he brought this kid home and it only turned out to be one of them darkies, didn't it?
DEBORAH   You're joking!
SIMONE   I got him right out of my house there and then. I'm not having it in my house. *(ANGELA enters. She directs this at her.)* Just because other people do it, don't mean I have to do it.
DEBORAH   I would have done the same thing and all.
JUSTINE   *(Referring to ANGELA.)* Look what the cat dragged in!
DEBORAH   I don't know how you've got the guts to sit round our table. I don't know what you're looking at me like that for pretending you don't know what I'm talking about.
SIMONE   She looks so smug doesn't she?
DEBORAH   I mean letting those coloured people in your house. I mean we are a community and we should stick together.
ANGELA   *(standing)* I think I'll have a gin.
(Three women sitting at next table overhear.)
WOMAN 1   Sure you don't want a brown ale! *(Everyone laughs.)*
ANGELA   I just don't see that it's any of your business.
DEBORAH   But we are a community!
ANGELA   They're only staying for a few days. They had nowhere else to go . . . just a few days. *(She exits.)*
DEBORAH   Well, that's what she says now. I mean a principle is a principle. She should not have let them in. *(She drinks her beer.)*
(The scene moves to ANGELA, at home. She is throwing the lodgers' belongings into a suitcase.)

ANGELA   Why should I be treated like this by the neighbours for people I hardly know? It just isn't fair. I tried to be helpful. I tried to be kind but they'll just have to go. They were nice people but it just won't work. They'll have to go. *(She throws their suitcase and other belongings outside her house into the street.)*
(The 'lodgers' arrive home.)
MOTHER   Oh God, Sharon. Oh Lord!
(The daughter rushes to the belongings strewn all over the street and picks up a soft toy. The mother knocks on ANGELA's door.)
MOTHER   Mrs Jones! Mrs Jones! Open the door!
(There is no answer and she returns to her daughter and starts to collect her belongings.)

Song *We'll survive*
DAUGHTER   Mama what we gonna do
MOTHER   Sweet baby, I don't know
   But we gotta stay together
DAUGHTER   Oh but mama I'm so cold
   I sometimes feel like I am dying
MOTHER   Sweet baby, my baby stop that crying
TOGETHER   Cause together, together, I know, and me we'll survive
(A series of period photographs appears on the screen [see Part One] while the entire company sing the second verse.)
ALL   What is this here England giving
   Sweet baby, it's my living
   But we cannot return home
   Oh but mama I'm so low
   I sometimes feel like I am dying
   Sweet baby — stop that crying
   Cause together, together, I know, and me we'll survive

Scene 9

INTERVIEWEE   You wouldn't give out your kids in the West Indies. The situation just couldn't arise. If you're married you're not going out to work because your husband's gone to work, so you stay home and look after the kids. But suppose you're a single girl and you have a baby and you don't get married. You carry it, take it to your mother or sister to say, 'Well I'm going to work, now you're family, you look after it.' It's not like here. Them just crafty. Them want the money and them don't want to look after the kids in the right way. After you carry your kids and come give them at morning time, you sit in that work worrying all day what's happening to them.
(Lights up on MRS BROWN, a childminder. She is sitting down knitting. There are scattered toys on the floor around her. There is a knock on the door. This slightly annoys her. She goes to answer it, and opens it to find MRS JOHNSON.)
MRS JOHNSON   Hello, Mrs Brown.
MRS BROWN   Mrs Johnson, why have you come back? Have you forgotten something?

MRS JOHNSON   No, I've just come to talk to you about Sharon.
MRS BROWN   Oh, well you better come in then. *(MRS JOHNSON follows her in.)* Would you like to sit down?
MRS JOHNSON   *(She sits.)* Thank you.
MRS BROWN   Is there anything wrong?
MRS JOHNSON   No, but it's this evening when I get Sharon home. She started to cry. You know when children sob. You know it upset me and I notice she was holding her back around this area. So I lift up her jumper and look and I see that ... I see a scratch like a bruise. And I was wondering where she could get that from Mrs Brown?
MRS BROWN   Well, I don't know. Well, she was alright today. She was playing quite happily with the other children.
MRS JOHNSON   Are you sure one of the children couldn't have hit her when you weren't in the room?
MRS BROWN   No, I was in the room all the day with her. I'm sorry, nothing happened ...
MRS JOHNSON   But you see, Mrs Brown, what concern my daughter concern me.
MRS BROWN   Yes, of course. But I'm sorry, I just can't help you. *(She stands.)*
MRS JOHNSON   *(She rises too.)* What is it with you childminders? I have a friend who was telling me just the other day that she took her child to the childminder's and found that she was in the same position in that pram. She hadn't been moved.
MRS BROWN   Has this got anything to do with me?
MRS JOHNSON   And another incident — the baby hadn't been changed all day. Just imagine that Mrs Brown!
MRS BROWN   Are you accusing me of something?
MRS JOHNSON   No, Mrs Brown.
MRS BROWN   Well, it certainly seems as if you are. Well now, you obviously don't trust me to look after your child. I think you better find someone else.
MRS JOHNSON   Listen, Mrs Brown.
MRS BROWN   Look, there's no need to raise your voice. . . .
MRS JOHNSON   My child has been crying, crying like she doesn't want to come back here. Now why do you tink that is Mrs Brown?
MRS BROWN   I just think that you should go and find someone else to look after your child.
MRS JOHNSON   *(She pauses to think, and then tries to reason with MRS BROWN, gently touching her hand.)* But Mrs Brown ...
MRS BROWN   *(She moves away from her.)* Just get out of my house.
MRS JOHNSON   Well, I tink I will. *(She starts for the door.)*
MRS BROWN   *(Moves to chair and sits.)* Before you go, just one more thing. Who are you gonna find to look after your child from so early in the morning till so late in the evening for so little pay?
MRS JOHNSON   *(Spends time thinking about this. Puts hand to head.)* I will see you the same time tomorrow morning Mrs Brown. *(She exits.)*

Scene 10

(A group of student nurses gather in a hospital corridor to find out examination results which have been posted.)

SIMONE I wonder what our results are. *(She looks at notices.)* I've passed!
ANGELA So have I!
EMELIA I've passed.
JUSTINE So have I.
EMELIA Let's go and tell the others.
(Enter CHRISTINE and LOUISA.)
LOUISA Oh no!
(They both look crestfallen as they realize that they have failed. CHERYL enters and looks.)
CHERYL See mine is there — 72!
CHRISTINE Yours is the one underneath that.
LOUISA You've got 42. I've got 41.
CHRISTINE I've got 42 as well.
LOUISA We're just going to have to try much harder.
(The nurses who have passed have all gathered in the background. Sister enters.)
SISTER Hello nurses.
NURSES Good morning Sister.
SISTER I'm here to congratulate you on your marks for your SEN exam. I'm so pleased. *(She smiles at those who have passed and turns to glare at those who have failed.)* Today you'll be going on to your new wards and you will be receiving your new badges, belts and caps. So please follow me.
SIMONE I wonder what new wards we'll be on. *(They exit.)*
CHRISTINE Just look at our marks next to theirs.
CHERYL It's not fair. I worked so hard.
LOUISA I expected it anyway.
CHERYL How do you mean you expected it anyway?
LOUISA Well, we just have to try much harder. If we get good marks they just push it down for us.
CHERYL So why didn't you tell me before and stop all that late night?
LOUISA It wouldn't have made any difference.
CHERYL It would have made difference to me. I didn't know people could be so wicked to other people.
(MATRON enters, and the girls stand straight in a row.)
NURSES Good morning matron.
MATRON What are you nurses doing standing around in this corridor?
CHERYL We were looking at our results, matron.
(MATRON examines results on notice board.)
MATRON Now I know why you're just standing around. You have no new wards to go to. Well, I suggest you're going to have to try much harder.
LOUISA We tried our best.
MATRON You could not have tried your best. Look at your marks next to the other nurses. You coloured girls think you can come from overseas and gain qualifications

without working hard. Well, I am very sorry to disappoint you all. Well, stop standing there and gazing at me and get to your wards. (*They exit.*)
(*Lights up on empty hospital room.*)
PATIENT'S VOICE Get your dirty black hands off me!
(*CHERYL runs in. She is in a distressed state. LOUISA follows. They both sit.*)
LOUISA Cheryl.
CHERYL Did you hear what she said to me Louisa? Did you hear?
LOUISA Just ignore them.
CHERYL Do you think it's nice? Do you think it nice?
LOUISA Cheryl, please.
CHERYL I can't ignore them. Them laughing at me, staring at me. I can't take it anymore. Anyway, I've made up my mind. I know what I'm going to do. I'm going to pack my bags. I'm going to leave.
LOUISA Cheryl, stop talking nonsense. You can't give up now. You've come all this way.
CHERYL Do you think I'm strong like you, Louisa?
LOUISA You will be.
CHERYL I won't be. You've got to be some kind of robot to live here. I can't take it anymore.
LOUISA Cheryl, please. People might be watching.
CHERYL So what if people are watching, Louisa? Why should I care now? Give me one good reason why I should care now? What hurts me so much is that I have to write these letters (*she takes one out of her pocket*) to my mother and father telling them what a lovely time I'm having. (*She reads.*) 'Dear Mother and Father, As usual I'm having a lovely time here.' Is that true Louisa?
LOUISA I write the same.
CHERYL 'Me and the nurses get on well.' Is that true Louisa? 'I passed my SEN with ease.' Is that true Louisa? 'And the matron love me off.' Is that true, is it? *She crumples the letter.*) If I was to write home to my mother and father and tell them the truth, no lies, they would die. They would just die. . . .
(*CHERYL cries, head in hands and LOUISA rises to comfort her.*)
Song *Unwelcome*
LOUISA No more tears
You've got to make the most of it
Life is hard, we know
Think of the future
When your children are older
Wiser the world we fall

They said to me, you'll find riches
They said to me the streets are gold
So I went on searching
But like a fool I was learning
We are different, life is different here
We are different, unwelcome

The people are cold

Like this place around me
Nowhere to go, no one
Five shillings, an empty pocket
Go to work, give the baby away
I pray everynight
Why is life one long fight
'Cos we're different, life is different here
We are different, unwelcome

Stop that crying
And forget your sorrow
Forget yesterday or regret tomorrow
Keep going strong. This war won't be too long

'Cos we're different, life is different here
We are different. Unwelcome
Unwelcome
Unwelcome

(*An excerpt from the Pathe newsreel 'Shameful Episode', 4 September 1958, describing the 'troubles' in Notting Hill in the summer of 1958 is shown.*)
NEWS ANNOUNCER   'Something new and ugly raises its head in Britain. In Notting Hill Gate, only a mile or two from London's West End, racial violence. An angry crowd of youths chases a negro into a greengrocer shop. While police reinforcements are called up to check the riot — one of the many that have broken out here in a few days — the injured victim, a Jamaican, is taken to safety. But the police have not been able to reach all the troubled spots so promptly and the quietest street may flare up in any moment.'

Scene 11

(*Six women enter, one at a time. It is the end of their long day and they are finally about to have a few minutes rest. Each one collapses into a chair, speaks her thoughts aloud and drifts off into sleep.*)
WOMAN 1   This is the first time I have had rest in weeks.
WOMAN 2   The only thing that keeps me going is fear.
WOMAN 3   I feel guilty; they make you feel it's your fault.
WOMAN 4   The thought of tomorrow reminds me of today; today reminds me of yesterday.
WOMAN 5   I feel as if I want to scream; this isn't what I came here for.
WOMAN 6   I'm tired; I'm so tired — I can sleep for a week.
(*There is an image of* ANGELA, *as interviewee on the screen, while the four dancers create a dream sequence depicting the life of one of the women in England. This is mixed with images of the other six women asleep. The song, the dance and the poem all go on simultaneously as the focus shifts from one to the other.*)
INTERVIEWEE   England

You know how I weep bitter tears for you
Everyday I watch this life this living
Eating my soul away
I see my reflection in the coldness of the mirror
Turning into a shadow of its former self and
Every wrinkle in my face
Every line that you see there
Each grey hair on my head represents
Another battle, another day, coped with
    conquered
All by myself, England
Is break you trying to break my spirit
Why you treat me so?
This weariness in my footsteps comes as much
From pain, bitterness, frustration, as it
    does from from weariness
And there is no one to see me
Cry invisible tears as I
Get up
Take them to school
Go to work
Come in
Feed them
Cook his dinner
Clean
Wash
Iron
Go to bed again and
Start all over again
    and again and again . . .

England

Song *Take me and hold me*
    Take me and hold me
    My neck is the place
    Your hand your people
    Your damn disgrace

    Free me and leave me
    No slave am I
    You free me, no loving
    Because with your love, you can lie

    I wanted to come
    And I thought this place was roses

Fascination stagnation
Pure hard white glass poses

Hold me
Control me
A robot for the cause
Sweep and clean
I'll follow your laws
My hands bear your scars
My children they rebel
You learn them your ways
So they rank till they smell

I wanted to come
England streets paved with gold
Fascination stagnation
England people have no soul

Take me hold me
My heart is the place
Your hand your people
Your blasted disgrace
I sit down I sigh
A slave I really am
You'll give me false love
Then for you England, I'll die.

Scene 12

INTERVIEWEE   Well, I couldn't stand the smell ... it seemed to be a completely different smell. I just couldn't understand why ... well habits y'know, just funny little habits like putting the bread — no paper on it — underneath the pram. Yes they never used to wrap the bread and if you go to the meatshop them wrap every damn ting in newspaper and we don't eat nothing out of newspaper in the West Indies — don't care how poor you are. In a way England was different to how I expected it, yes because when you see those English people going over there looking so posh and nice ... and you come here and see how them live, well y'know it was a shock to me ...

(*Lights up at bus stop. Two groups of women, dressed for church and carrying their bibles are seen talking.*)

SYLVIA   Good morning, Sister Beverley. Is how you be? (*They shake hands.*)
BEVERLEY   I be alright Sister Sylvia and how is you?
SYLVIA   Fine.
BEVERLEY   That's good. That's good. Praise the Lord.
SYLVIA   So what did you tink of the church service this morning?
BEVERLEY   It was really good you know. I really enjoy it. And that preacher man. I tell

you, he can really preach good.
SYLVIA   It's true. I wonder where that bus can be. It's taking its time.
BEVERLEY   Y'know the service, them bad on Sunday.
(GLENIS enters.)
BEVERLEY   Sister Glenis!
GLENIS   Sister Sylvia! *(They shake hands.)*
SYLVIA   How you be?
GLENIS   Not too bad, living another day, and Sister Russell?
BEVERLEY   How you be, Sister Glenis?
GLENIS   Well fine, fine y'know, but living another day of course.
BEVERLEY   That's good. Praise the Lord!
SYLVIA   Did I see you in church this morning?
GLENIS   Of course.
BEVERLEY   Me see her. Me see her.
GLENIS   Yes, I did just go down the road, just to get a few tings. Of course I was in church today, man. That preacher the way him preached. He give you the strength to go on y'know, to see another day.
BEVERLEY   It's true.
SYLVIA   I was just about to say to Sister Beverley.
BEVERLEY   What's that?
SYLVIA   I tink it's the pressing that's growing her hair. She was bald before y'know.
BEVERLEY   No man! I tell you seh it's not the pressing that's growing my hair. It's the way that preacher man preach. I tell you when him preach the words just vibrate and my head a shoot out. Look! It cyan stop growin'.
GLENIS   That's why you must praise God y'know. A good psalm to read is this one. *(She shows them in her bible.)*
(Focus switches to second group of women.)
SANDRA   Did I tell you 'bout my back? How it used to be so bad and everyting? Well, me go to the Bishop of the church the other day and he put his hand 'pon my back and him bless it and it's better now.
LOUISA   Praise God.
SAMANTHA   What you must do is buy your own bokkle of water make him bless it for you and put it 'pon your back, a good ting that y'know . . .
LOUISA   It's true, yes. One time I did hear a story y'know about a woman she couldn't walk at all y'know. Anyway, them take her to the Bishop of the church and now she can walk like anyting.
SANDRA   That really good. D'you see her? She gawn in a spirit the other day. She a shoutin' and praising Lord and everyting.
SAMANTHA   So long as you believe in the Lord anyting can happen.
(A woman walks past the bus stop, carrying a loaf of bread under her arm. All the women watch her pass in amazement!)
SAMANTHA   Oh Jesus!
SANDRA   Oh my Lord!
SAMANTHA   The bread under the armpit! It must a stink.
SANDRA   Y'know what? Them even dig out the milk bottle top and nyam out the cream,

the children them.
SAMANTHA   We was walking past this house one time and me see the bread 'pon the doorstep, no paper on it. One dog come along and cock up a foot and piss 'pon the bread, piss 'pon the bread same way.
LOUISA   Them even wrap them food in paper y'know, newspaper.
(A mother enters with her child lagging behind.)
CHILD   Mum, you're walking too fast and I'm tired.
MOTHER   *(Stops and looks at child.)* Tina, you're such a slow coach. Oh my God, look on your face! *(She spits on her hands and cleans her daughter's face. The women express horror to each other.)*
SAMANTHA   Y'see what the woman did to the pickney face?
GLENIS   My sisters, back home my father wouldn't hawk and spit 'pon the dog like that.
BEVERLEY   It's true.
SAMANTHA   That's where them get them spots from.
LOUISA   Them is disgusting!
SYLVIA   And nasty them nasty!

Song *Here in my motherland*

ALL
As I step off the boat and I look at the city
I lift up my hand and say 'Oh, what a pity',
To leave my country and to come to this land
Oh how I wish I was not in England

The buildings were dirty, mash up and old
If only it wasn't so dark and so cold
Then maybe I would want to live this life through
Here in my motherland, what else can I do?

SYLVIA   Dirty, dirty place, don't you tink?
LOUISA   With them sausage and sauce and them fish and chip stink.
SANDRA   Me husband put on him three quarter trousers you see.
But the English just point and start laugh after him.
BEVERLEY   It's not a nice place fe live or to be.
If only me could see Jamaica palm tree.
GLENIS   Them nasty in ways that I could not laugh.
SAMANTHA   I don't even tink them wash or them bath.
ALL   My life was so sweet before I did leave
Oh Jesus help me, help me to see.

As I step off the boat and I look at the city, etc. *(Repeat chorus.)*
(The women start dancing now, as they sing the chorus, on their own and with each other.)
SYLVIA   Them write me from home and I write them back.
LOUISA   But what I did send them was not the true fact.
SANDRA   That living in England is hard and so rough.
BEVERLEY   Me know now that I have had more than enough.
GLENIS   I sometimes sit down and wonder what's next.
SAMANTHA   This life that I'm leading is making me vex!

ALL   But true seh we have to live this life through.
     Here in my Motherland what else can I do?

(As chorus is repeated, the women get more absorbed in dancing and dance to another chorus of music.)

SAMANTHA   Lord, look how you made me miss the bus! *(They all stop and run off to catch the bus.)*

Scene 13

INTERVIEWEE   I think in every race it's always the women who hold things together. I know in the West Indian house the man comes in and he sits and it's the woman who makes the arrangements and does the planning and brings up the children and she plans, she decides when they should buy a house and decides the school the kids should go to and she has retained all her West Indianness. It is always the women who make the decisions about everything to do with the family and in this country the women came and they decided they couldn't live in these terrible conditions and so this saving to go home in two years time had to go because they needed the houses to live in and it was the woman who decided on that. *(Lights upon three women. Each is standing in her own space facing the audience.)*

WOMAN 1   We had to keep moving all the time. I said to you I think we'd be better off trying to save for a house. The children are growing up now and it's not nice to be bringing two kids up in one room; four people sleeping on one room you know. You need a paraffin heater to keep you warm; you've got to dry the washing or there was no heating otherwise. The smell. All the struggle. I keep thinking this isn't going to get anywhere. Somedays I have thought it is not worth living. I come from work, wash the nappies, cook the dinner, watch that they don't turn over the paraffin heater. If you were ambitious we might have been able to own a house by now. I asked you: 'Why don't we try to save for a house?' You said: 'I can do without a house all I want is a car.' We needed two of us; we needed two. Without your help we couldn't get anywhere. It was always one room, one room, until the kids were going to school and it was still one room. As soon as your car is squashed you buy another one; that's all you can think about.

WOMAN 2   The least thing you were ready to hit me and things like that. I never lived with a man before. I never knew what your nature was. From the time I came over you began to use me as a slave. Like you sent for me to be a slave. We couldn't get on. It just gets worse. When I got home from work one evening I found that you weren't there. I didn't see most of your things in the room. You didn't leave any message, nothing. You even took the television. I am left on my own with two kids. I feel relief.

WOMAN 3   Do you remember when you sent for me? How carefully we planned it all. You would go first and then I would join you. We had our family young and all four children were to be left behind with your mother, so we could concentrate on working hard and saving. We were so ambitious. We worked and saved and bought our house, our own little house, we did it up lovely. As soon as that was done I saved and saved to send for the kids. I would send for them one by one. How I trusted you. Our wages were quite small but still we were managing. We were just about to send for the third child. And then came the day that changed everything. I remember it was snowing. I had just come home from work to see the council in the house throwing out everything. They told me the mortgage had been so much in arrears. I couldn't believe it. Then they said, 'I'm so sorry, Mrs, but your husband borrowed so much off the house.' Why? I ask you why? I was paying for everything. I was taking no housekeeping money from you. I even paid for the deposit on the house. I mean what did you do with it? How did you spend it? How could you after we tried so hard? Sometimes I wonder how I never went mad. After all the struggles we went through ...

Song *You have changed*
WOMAN 3   I remember when we used to walk the sunny island of Jamaica
          We used to laugh and we used to hide
          We used to want to be together
          and bonded forever
          Oh yes but you have changed a lot
          You have changed a lot
          You have changed a lot
          Yes I think so.

          All you do, all you do is go to work
          You come back in demand this and that
          Sit down there and read that damn paper
          Avoid your children and avoid me
          Oh yes you have changed a lot
          You have changed a lot
          You have changed a lot
          Yes I know so.

WOMAN 1   I might as well live on my own. When we think we've had enough we're quick to find a way out. I've had enough. I don't want to know.
WOMAN 2   Why should a woman sit and let a man get her down? I try for myself. I get the money myself. I don't wait for him to say 'I'll give it to you next week or the week to come'. Everything I've done, I've done for myself.
WOMAN 3   A lot of us are on our own now. I'll never take another man in my life again; I'll never marry again. I'm happier on my own.

Scene 14

(Lights up on MARCIA *and her* MOTHER, *sitting exactly as in Scene 1.)*
MOTHER   I stopped thinking of England as this mother country after the first year, after the first couple of months. I still don't feel that I belong. I mean, after all these years, and after all this work, yes I've been paid, but I have worked so hard and I've put up with a hell of a lot. So now they say that I'm supposed to be part of this community, feel

part of the community, but still I know that if someone out there decided to be nasty to me I just couldn't take it. I suppose on the surface I would lash out at them, yes. But deep down the sense of belonging is not there. And it's this that I tried to prepare you for, Marcia, in the way that I grow you.
(She takes the tape out of the cassette recorder and hands it over to Marcia.)
So is this what you wanted? The interview?
(Lights up on entire company, appearing as they did in Scene 2, but this time in groups of mother and daughter. Each pair or small group is engaged in some activity, e.g. mother plaiting daughter's hair as they sing:)

ALL   England, sweet England
       Is dere we gwine live
       The air is so different
       But our labour we a give
       Even though we know
       (Even though we know)
       The difference is big
       Sweet England, we comin to live.

(The company hum as the mothers speak.)
MOTHER 1   The way I did it is to give my children the best education they can have. I think it's very important; education is a lifelong thing, once you've got it no one can take that away from you.
MOTHER 2   I taught them not to feel that just because they were born in London they are more special than the person who comes up from the West Indies because in the long run they are going to be treated just the same.
MOTHER 3   I survive only by the strength of the Lord. I said to my children and other young people, 'Seek the Lord while you are young for that's the only way to survive in England.'
MOTHER 4   I bring up my child just as how I would bring her up in the West Indies. I tell her how my mum grow me. I have to tell her the ways of the people over here are different. You have to be very careful how you move amongst people.
MOTHER 5   I tried not to fight their battles for them but to prepare them for coming up against prejudice. So I try to make them feel proud of being black and to give them as much as possible some values, and to teach them about their background.
MARCIA'S MOTHER   *(to audience)* She don't understand. I sometimes remember talking to her and going upstairs to my room crying because it's so darn unfair. No matter how we try to prepare them, it's never enough. They have to go through it, they have to . . . I don't accept it, and I won't accept it.

Song *You don't know*
(Lights up on MARCIA *at the piano.)*
MARCIA   I know you're not a child
       I can't tell you what to do
       but I can tell you
       all the things that I've been through
       I fear today for what tomorrow holds

for what you don't yet know
but must soon begin to feel

You don't know
You don't know
You don't know
but I'm telling you

You're born here it's true
you know the people's ways
but I'm so afraid girl
they will never let you belong
I can see you're different
— you won't accept the things we did
But I'm scared when you talk like that
of what your future holds

ALL THE MOTHERS
    I know you're not a child
    I wouldn't tell you what to do
    but I'd like to teach you, tell you
    everything I'm going through
    There's so much you don't know
    you got to realize
    a black woman in this land
    you must fight to survive
    and so to help you
    I give you my life
    my experience too
    I hope you can make it through

Part Three
THE DRAMA LESSONS

The third and final part of this book contains ten basic dramatic structures that can be used in conjunction with the earlier sections in Part One. Each structure contains ideas for several lessons. Throughout, drama is used as the principal method of learning. Many of the strategies were used, together with the primary sources and testimony, in creating *Motherland*. Others were devised throughout the second year of the project as the *Motherland* materials were tried out in a number of different schools*. Much of this work was carried out with history and social studies teachers and other non-drama specialists as well as with drama teachers.

AN APPROACH TO DRAMA

The outline of work contained in this section represents a distinct approach to drama. This approach is characterized by the following features:

1 *Collaborative learning* Drama relies upon the willingness of pupils and teacher to identify actively with the drama situation and work effectively with the group as a whole.

2 *Dramatic conventions* Drama offers a wide range of conventions and devices to which pupils can be introduced through their active involvement in improvisatory work.

3 *Social content* Drama offers a rare opportunity for pupils to explore issues of value relating to important social and political topics.

That last element is of particular significance, especially with regard to any attempt at exploring racism and sexism through drama. Themes surrounding these issues become repetitive and superficial when approached primarily at the level of subjective feeling and intuition. It seems to me that any approach which fails to introduce an element of fact, personal testimony and political analysis leaves us teaching pupils no more than they in fact already know. We thus fail to give them the tools with which to gain an altered perspective that would affect their lives and bring about personal and political change. It is essential, however, that the information given should be open to critical interpretation by the pupils themselves. It is by means of this process that drama becomes a record of the pupils' urge towards a greater understanding of issues that are at once intensely personal and deeply social.

CHOOSING MATERIALS

The criteria for choosing material will vary according to subject and focus. I tend to choose material that falls into at least one of five categories: *factual material* that might help to inform the drama; *dilemmas* that would confront the pupils with the

---

*I am particularly grateful to the History Department of Vauxhall Manor School for trying out many of these materials as part of their third-year course — 'People on the Move to Britain'.

problems that are faced or have been faced by others; *vivid images* that could be used to heighten the drama and sometimes provide a focus for it; *analysis* of a particular issue that would help to place the work in a wider context; and *personal testimony* that records the individual struggles, the triumphs and the frustrations of other people's lives. It is the introduction of authentic personal accounts into the lesson that impresses pupils most profoundly on an emotional level with the knowledge that the work they are doing is based on real situations and the experience of real people.

BASIC STRATEGIES

Although all the strategies used are explained within the context of the lessons, two are of special significance and require some explanation from the outset.

The play within the play

Many drama specialists make a distinction between drama as a process of learning and theatre as an end product. However, in recent years these two approaches have been brought closer together with the recognition that many drama teachers use theatrical elements in their work, even if this is not directed towards polished performance. Pupils enjoy 'showing' and presentation can be used to highlight, emphasize, or focus on a particular aspect of the material.

I always try to ensure that the 'showing' is made as much a part of the context of the drama as possible. The device of the play within the play is helpful in this respect. It allows the pupils to adopt a spectator role within the broader framework of the improvised drama; it incorporates the presentation into the explorative process. For example, in lesson 2, each group is asked to present its farewells and its final moments of parting as a ceremony that is being celebrated as part of their going-away party. It is important to note that this device requires a prior understanding by the pupils of the kind of drama they are operating. They themselves need to understand and appreciate the convention.

Teacher in role

By taking a role in the drama, as opposed to remaining on the outside as spectator or observer, it is possible for the teacher to alter the structure and movement of the lesson from within the fictional context. By adopting a role appropriate to the situation it is possible for the teacher to set up and develop drama experiences for the whole class working together in one group. This is perhaps the most useful device in terms of being able to introduce background information into the drama and therefore requires careful planning and the memorization of information beforehand.

Teachers who have not previously worked in this way may experience some initial difficulty. If this is a new experience for you and your pupils it may prove helpful to tell them in advance what you intend to do and to explain the kinds of roles you are going to adopt. These may correspond closely to your teaching role or be very different. The choice of role is all important and needs considerable forethought and a willingness to experiment. This device may not work immediately with every class. However, as a class becomes more familiar with this technique it can prove highly successful.

Lesson 1 Reasons for Leaving

DRAMATIC STRUCTURE

1. *Small-group work*
   Divide into family groups of 4–5. Establish relationships within the family. Use the occasion of a typical evening meal to allow pupils time to develop their roles.

2. *Whole-group work*
   Each of the families is invited to a meeting at the local village hall. They are told that a representative of Her Majesty's Government will be speaking about the prospects of migration to England.

3. *Small-group work*
   Returning to their family groups after the meeting, each group is to discuss what they think are the advantages and disadvantages of migrating to England. They may want to make a list for themselves.

4. *Small-group work*
   Teacher asks each group to prepare a short scene showing *one* incident that occurs to members of the family that helps them decide that at least one of them must migrate to Britain. They should be encouraged to show the moment that clinches the decision. Each group shows its work to the other groups.

INFORMING THE DRAMA

Teacher explains details of the family's situation: they live on a small West Indian island, shortly after the Second World War (1953). (You may wish to refer to background notes in Section I, Part One, p. 5.)

Teacher in role as representative of the British Government outlines the advantages of moving to Britain. As a native of the 'Mother Country' she can answer questions about the quality of life there and encourages the group to ask questions.

Teacher in role visits each group and points out the advertisement (Part One, Section I) for cheap fares to Britain. In these meetings with the smaller group, her role is to allay any further doubts or suspicions they might have about coming to Britain.

The work is informed through discussion and evaluation of what has already happened to the family.

POINTERS

It needs to be made clear that it is a struggle for the family to obtain the necessities for living.

They live in a small village community and their occupations might include shopkeeping, agriculture or light industry.

It is possible that the pupils will view the situation from their present perspective. They may be cynical about the job opportunities outlined by the speaker in light of the present economic situation. The teacher may wish to stop the drama here to discuss the differences between the 50s and 80s and then begin again.

The advertisements are taken from the Jamaican *Daily Gleaner* of 1955. The use of primary sources such as these in the actual drama helps to make immediate the original context.

The group may want to re-read the testimonies in Section I to help them with their discussion and evaluation.

It has been said that a combination of *economic circumstances* in the country of origin (the West Indies) and *economic prospects* in the country of settlement (Britain) is one of the major causes of migration.

'Push' and 'pull' factors are often distinguished in the literature on the causes of migration. Some of these could be fed into the drama by the teacher (using the teacher-in-role strategy) in her talks with the potential migrants.

Push Factors
— Deterioration of economic conditions since Second World War
— Overpopulation
— Natural disasters e.g. floods and hurricanes
— Underemployment
— Unemployment
— Low wages
— Lack of educational and vocational opportunities

Pull Factors
— Economic boom in Britain since Second World War
— Year-round jobs e.g. London Transport, National Health Service
— Higher wages
— Better opportunities for educational and vocational training
— Cheap fares
— View of Britain as mother country
— Britain has an open door policy whereas the USA (a traditional destination for migrants from the West Indies) had limited entry from 1952

Lesson 2 Preparing and Parting

DRAMATIC STRUCTURE

1 *Whole-group work*
Families arrive at village school for a farewell party. Each family arrives at the local school house where all the people from the village who are going over to England are given a 'traditional send-off'.

2 *Whole-group work — farewell speeches*
The party organizer begins the speeches by saying goodbye to those members of the community who are leaving. They are asked to stand.

3 *Small-group work*
Each family group is asked to prepare a short scene which will be performed as part of the farewell ceremony in which members of a family say goodbye to the person who is leaving. As part of this ritual, each member of the family must offer the leaver a gift to take to Britain and some words of advice. The person who is leaving responds to the gift and the advice.

4 *Whole-group work*
The farewell ceremony at the village school is resumed. Each group presents its play as part of the celebration.

INFORMING THE DRAMA

Teacher in role, as teacher of the village school and party organizer, greets each family; confirms who is leaving and generally creates a party atmosphere. She offers food and helps the families to share their experiences with each other.

Teacher in role uses testimony (Part One, Section 2, p. 16) to explain how people she has known in the past have felt about leaving.

Background notes and testimony (Part One, Section 2) can be used here.

The play within the play
The presentation of each play is coordinated by the teacher in role who links the different scenes and brings the party to an end.

POINTERS

Many of the women who were interviewed spoke of a party the night before people went off to England. In this lesson the village school is used as a means of bringing all the families together.

In this kind of whole-group work, it is essential that each group be given a specific task: e.g.

1. Find out the reasons for leaving of at least one other family.
2. As a reporter on the local paper, interview members who are leaving about their feelings.

This is another opportunity for the teacher in role to review the reasons for leaving and to highlight how some of the women felt about parting. Pupils should be encouraged to respond in role.

She may also use this speech to inform further about

Raising money for fares
Leaving children behind
Intentions to return after a few years

(See background notes, Part One, Section 2.)

Alternatively the group can be asked to create a tableau or short scene focussing on a word or phrase taken from the women's testimony.

Some examples of key words and phrases:

'It was a very emotional time'.
'Too painful to part'.
'Overwhelmed'.
'If you have to go, you just have to go'.
'Lost for words'.

The group may wish to go on to prepare an additional scene showing in more naturalistic terms the final moments in which the members of the family are together before they part.

'I had to come from Kingston and stop at Port Antonio with my family. Then the following morning my whole family go down to the wharf ... some cry.'

Lesson 3 First Impressions

DRAMATIC STRUCTURE

1 *Whole-group work*
A meeting of trainee newspaper reporters with their editors. The year is 1955 and the mass arrival of migrants from the West Indies is making big news. The trainee reporters are briefed about covering the event and are given their initial assignment. (The paper plans to run a series about the new arrivals.)

2 *Pair work*
Pupils conduct their interviews and take notes. In pairs, pupils may swap roles as interviewer and interviewee.

3 *Whole-group work*
Meeting of the reporters with their editors to discuss the interviews that have just taken place.

4 *Small-group work*
In small groups, the pupils are asked to choose an incident or experience that they feel will make a good human interest story for the newspaper. They are then to prepare this as a short scene.

5 *Whole group — showing the improvised scenes*
Each group presents its scene to the rest of the class.

INFORMING THE DRAMA

Teacher in role as 'editor' talks to the trainees about the arrival of the 'boat-trains'. She gives them details about the situation the migrants find themselves in when they arrive. She refers to Testimony (Part One, Section 3).

Taking notes
These notes will be fed back into the lesson in the next phase in order to inform the drama. (See below.)

Discussion in role
Reporters are asked for comments about their interviews. By referring to their notes, they are asked to report back on some of the things they have discovered. Teacher in role as editor can chair the discussion.

Consolidation
The small groups can use any of the testimony, literature and their own notes to help them prepare the scene.

Teacher as narrator The teacher can link the scenes by means of a short commentary that will relate them to the theme as a whole.

POINTERS

The group will need to discuss the kinds of questions they will want to ask the newcomers and the kind of notes they will need to take.

In role the teacher can instruct the trainees as to the best way of going about reporting tasks e.g. Trainees should be encouraged not to write everything down that the interviewee says but only the most interesting and/or the most unusual statements.

The actual task of taking notes will need to vary depending on the age and ability of the group. With younger pupils it may be necessary to ask each 'reporter' to jot down three or four key phrases that represent the migrants' first impressions of Britain.

Alternatives to working in pairs:

1. Working in groups of three, one pupil is the interviewee, another conducts the interview, while another takes notes.
2. A group interview — the whole class asks questions to the teacher in role as the newly-arrived migrant. (In this case one or more pupils can be given the task of taking notes.)

This gives an opportunity for the group to pool their ideas and impressions.

This session needs to be speedy, brief and to the point.

Pupils no longer have roles specified e.g. interviewer/interviewee. Now they must choose their own new roles as they become the characters in the human interest story.

The following passages from Edward Scobie's *Black Britannia* provide a useful link between scenes:

> They came by the boatload, and by chartered flights to Britain. They sold, bartered, stole and saved to make the journey to their promised land.
>
> They came in their lightweight suits and straw hats ... teeth chattering, shivering in the draughty, freezing, alien, impersonal, busy atmosphere of the railway stations.
>
> Waterloo, Victoria, Charing Cross or anywhere else they were dumped together with the cardboard boxes and battered suitcases.

This device can be used in one of two ways. The teacher can link each scene by summing up the points of the previous scene and introducing the next *or* she can read from other source material that describes the arrival of West Indian migrants.

105

Lesson 4 Housing

DRAMATIC STRUCTURE

1 *Whole-group work*
   Pupils are divided into two groups: half are landladies/lords; the other half are those who have just arrived in Britain with all of their belongings. The landladies are in a fixed position around the room. Those taking on the role of the migrants are asked to walk the streets looking for accommodation.

2 *Pair work*
   Each migrant is asked to stop at the door of a landlady and to try and obtain accommodation. They may have to explain their situation: how they knew there was a vacancy, whether they have children, a job, etc.

3 *Repetition of whole-group work/pair work (as above)*
   This is repeated several times alternating from the narration to the encounters and back to the narration as the pupils continue to walk the streets, knocking on several different doors in search of accommodation.

4 *Small-group work — prepared improvisation*
   In small groups the pupils are asked to prepare a short scene that demonstrates *one* of the problems that the new tenants have with their landlords once they have moved in.

5 *Presentation of the prepared scenes*
   Each group presents its scene to the others. They are told to remain in their positions when the scene is finished for further questioning.

INFORMING THE DRAMA

Repetition of narrative
As the arrivals are walking the streets, teacher, as narrator, reads repeatedly excerpts from testimony describing first impressions of Britain and the search for housing.

Teacher explains why so many people were turned away at the time — she can refer to background notes which describe housing situations in the 1950s.

Teacher advises As the mood changes and those searching for housing become more frustrated, the teacher can alter her instructions to the landladies. They can offer substandard accommodation with many restrictions.

Pupils are asked to study the testimony and background notes before preparing the scene. This should provide them with lots of examples of the difficulties in the area of housing experienced by many of the migrants.

Pupils as experts
Each pupil in the scene is asked to respond to questions from the rest of the class, still maintaining the role that he/she played in the scene. The rest of the class are instructed to ask questions that will clarify the situation presented in the scene.

POINTERS

It may help to darken the room in order to intensify the atmosphere. The simple device of just repeating certain passages from the testimony can intensify the mood. You may choose your own passage or use some from the testimony or play.

'It was very cold ... everywhere looked strange; the buildings were grey.... The houses are like prisons. I noticed the grey dull buildings ... how wet and dark everywhere is ... I couldn't believe it ... seeing houses without verandahs ... I couldn't believe it was London ... it was really cold.'

Landladies may be taken aside and briefed separately. They may be told to say *no* at this point but there may be different ways to refuse accommodation e.g. polite, aggressive, awkward ...

George Lamming describes a situation of a migrant approaching the house where she read there was a room for rent: 'You knew that the answer had to be given there and then. And the answer was often long, circuitous, a marathon of courtesies that ended with regret that the room, like a bird, had just gone. Of course it was still there and empty too.' (*The Pleasures of Exile*, 1960.)

The teacher can vary the instructions to the landladies as the drama progresses. The pupils need to recognize that even when offered accommodation, it often will be substandard, overpriced or with many restrictions. Teacher may ask landladies and migrants to swap roles, to offer each a chance to experience both situations.

Some restrictions tenants might face
— Use of kitchen and toilet facilities during certain hours only
— No noise (children to be kept quiet!)
— No added furniture or electrical appliances
— Lights at certain times only
— In by 10.00 pm
— Restricted visitors
— Paying rent in advance

Most of the interviewees spoke of difficulties with landlords and landladies when trying to pinpoint the problems they experienced living in a particular accommodation. This relationship between tenant and landlord is central to the issue being explored here.

This requires the pupil to think in role and on her feet about some aspect of the situation she did not consider before. It can create a deeper understanding of the context of the situation and help us to understand more about the motivations of some of the characters they have created.

Pupils may need some examples of the kinds of questions to be asked. The teacher can join in the questioning, e.g. How did you feel towards the landlady when she told you to shut out the light? How did these restrictions affect other areas of your life, (e.g. your relationship with your children)?

Lesson 5 Earning a Living

DRAMATIC STRUCTURE

1 *In pairs*
Each of the pupils is asked to take on the role of someone who has recently arrived in Britain from the West Indies and is just starting work in a food-processing factory (e.g. Walls, Lyons, Peak Freans) in the 1950s. They introduce themselves and discuss their hopes and fears with another migrant.

2 *Whole-group work — 'special induction meeting'*
Having been told that they will attend a special induction meeting, the pupils are asked to prepare the room for this. In role, they listen to the talk by the personnel officer (teacher in role) and respond with any questions they have.

3 *Small-group work — prepared improvisation*
Working in groups of 4–5, the pupils are asked to prepare a short scene that will take place when the 'newcomers' are trained for work by the 'old timers'. This should include *an incident* that will highlight some of the tensions that might exist between them.

4 *Small-group work — presented improvisation*
Each group shows its scene which demonstrates an incident of tension. The teacher and the rest of the class question those in the scene — remaining in role — further.

INFORMING THE DRAMA

Teacher explains that during the 1950s Cracker Snaps, another large food firm, held special induction courses for their West Indian workers. She explains that the company they will be working for will have a similar policy towards their West Indian workers. They may want to discuss their feelings about that in role.

Teacher in role as personnel officer welcomes the 'newcomers' to the firm. She explains that this meeting is specifically for 'foreign workers' because there have been 'misunderstandings' in the past. She sets out the rules they must observe and opens the meeting up for questions. They are told they will be shown their routines by some of the 'old timers'.

The incident can be taken from any idea in the *testimony* or *background notes* or based on any of the misunderstandings about the rules stated at the induction meeting. The teacher may want to discuss beforehand some of the tensions that might arise.

Questioning role
When *questioning* those in the scene, the teacher and pupils may want to take on the roles of management or trade union representatives investigating the incident.

POINTERS

The informal meeting in pairs gives the pupils some time to think about their roles. It is also important that they should be given some indication that as West Indian workers they will be treated differently by the firm.

Most of the workers would have found out about the jobs through friends at the factory or through the employment exchange.

There was a 10 per cent quota on the employment of West Indian workers in many factories at the time.

The teacher, in role as 'personnel officer', may be quite friendly on the surface but will be very firm about the rule directed towards the 'newcomers' — she should somehow make the newcomer feel uncomfortable. The teacher may want to hand out a list of rules in the form of a letter or read it out to the workers.

The rules listed here are based on interviews with personnel officers at Cracker Snaps and at Pan-Provisions between 1955—8 (Patterson, 96—101)

'Adapt' yourselves and 'behave' like anybody else!
No fighting. No lateness.
Dress like everyone else.
Women must not keep hats on indoors.
Do not bring own food to eat in the canteen.
The importance of hygiene and cleanliness always stressed in food handling.
Don't get pregnant. (There was a large turnover through pregnancy.)

The teacher may want to insert a preliminary exercise where the pupils simply practise the tasks they are to perform on the job.

It is important to try and avoid a stereotypical response to the 'newcomers' by the British workers. Surely there was discrimination and racist abuse, but there was also increased understanding and genuine friendships created for some.

It is also important to avoid an unsubtle response by the group playing the 'newcomers'. They too may have ambivalent feelings about their relationships with some of the 'old timers'.

Other factors
No more than 25 per cent of 'coloured workers' were ever put in one department.

A department could choose not to have black employees.

There were informal leaders referred to as 'old stagers' who helped to smooth things out within the group.

The questioning in role may help to break down this kind of response. The incident may be directed towards a few by a few. What tensions might this create in those not directly involved?

Lesson 6 Childcare

DRAMATIC STRUCTURE

1 *Small-group work — discussion*
In groups of 4–5, discuss the various dilemmas that the women had to face about working and looking after their children. Pupils are asked to 'choose *one* dilemma that you think is particularly significant — one that you might like to develop further'.

2 *Small-group work — dramatic moments*
In the same groups of 4–5, each group is asked to prepare and show a tableau or still photograph that illustrates the dilemma it has chosen.

3 *Whole-group work*
The class discuss all the dilemmas that they have seen. They are asked to choose *one* that they would all wish to continue to work on. (A vote may be taken.)

4 *Small-group work — prepared improvisation*
Having chosen one woman's situation the pupils go back to their original groups to prepare a scene that will show how the dilemma facing the woman over childcare will affect one other area of her life.

5 *Whole-group work — presentation of scenes*
The group whose situation they have chosen to focus upon repeats its original tableau. Each group presents its scene.

INFORMING THE DRAMA

Teacher reviews some of the difficulties the women had over childcare by referring to notes and testimony.

Teacher advises the group to choose a moment that will enable the rest of the class to see one of the basic conflicts facing the woman (e.g. a woman arrives at a childminder's home to discover some children being mistreated — freeze).

Teacher explains that they will *all* be working on *one* of the women's situations that they have discussed so far. They must choose one that they would like to study in more depth.

By referring to testimony and notes, *teacher relates* the other areas of the woman's life that have been affected by her responsibility for childcare (e.g. one of the women decided to give up full-time work).

Teacher as narrator — the teacher can use a narrative link to relate each sequence.

POINTERS

You may prefer to get pupils to draw up a list of the various dilemmas on a large piece of sugar paper.

Some difficulties faced by many of the women:
How do you find suitable childcare facilities?
What do you do if you find your child is being mistreated?
How do you cope with the pressures of both work and childcare?
What do you do if a child is ill?
What do you do to ease your exhausting routine?
Should you accept a part-time job or one with less responsibility in order to be able to coordinate the job with childcare?
How do you pay for childminding out of a low wage?

This work should be brief (5—10 minutes in preparation). The pupils are asked to focus on a single image in order to present their ideas to the whole class. A tableau or a still photograph can highlight the basic attitudes and tensions in a given situation.

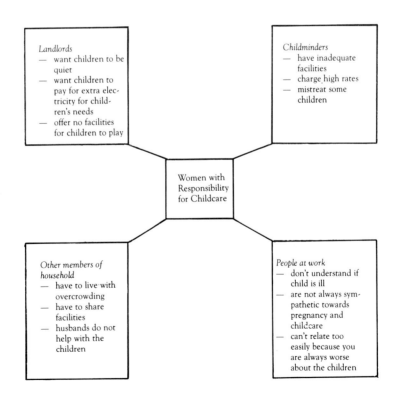

111

Lesson 7 Relationships with Men

DRAMATIC STRUCTURE

1 *In pairs*
Discuss with a friend how the pressures of life in England are affecting your relationships at home.

2 *Small-group work*
Break up into family groups of 4–5. Discuss relationships and problems brought about by the move to England. Act out an incident amongst yourselves that will highlight some of the pressures being put on the relationship.

3 *Whole-group work*
The couple from each family group are asked to discuss some of their problems with each other in role. They will each do this in front of the whole group.

4 *Small-group work — photographs*
Each group is asked to prepare three photographs or tableaux:

1 to depict the relationship within the family before they emigrated;
2 after being in England for some time;
3 after the marriage has broken down.

5 *Whole-group work*
Presentation of three photographs from each group.

INFORMING THE DRAMA

Teacher *explains* by summing up some of the experiences that have been explored in previous sections.

How might these pressures affect a marriage?

Review all the testimony on this topic to help with ideas for the incident.

Doubling
Two others from the same group are asked to speak as the inner voices of the couple. So we hear from the first pair what the couple are saying to each other and from the second pair what the couple are *really* thinking.

Pupils may wish to look at the song 'You have changed' in Scene 13 of *Motherland* (p. 95). This might help to get a sense of how the relationship changed throughout the different experiences.

Questioning in role
Members of the class ask questions to each family group in role about any details in the photographs or aspects of the situation that are unclear.

POINTERS

Each person should be given a few minutes to talk about their relationships and then to listen to a friend. This exercise is used as a means of getting the pupils to focus on the pressures put on the relationships in England.

'In those early days, you could only look to your husband. If he's not ambitious, there's no way you can make it with two small children.'

The group may want to focus on one of the underlying causes to the breakdown of relationships i.e. the changing roles of men and women in this country.

'We come from a society where men were always the providers. I suppose that would create a lot of problems because the women were working here. They're more independent.'

This device may help the group identify some of the ways in which the couple are not communicating.

Pupils may need a fair bit of instruction in using this device i.e. the husband speaks to the wife — his double voices his inner thoughts; the wife replies — her double voices her inner thoughts.

'I'd never lived with a man before so I didn't know what his nature was like. It was hard for us to talk about it.'

By creating photographs, the pupils are attempting to create an image that may immediately express the changing attitudes within the family.

'A lot of women reckoned their husbands changed when they came to England.'

The group may prefer to concentrate on the situation experienced by one of the families.

'People don't leave each other so much in Jamaica.'

Lesson 8 Responses to the 'New Community'

DRAMATIC STRUCTURE

1 *Whole-group work*
A meeting takes place to set up a new community organization. Its purpose is to bring about better understanding between the migrant and the British people. Local people have been invited representing both sections of the community. (The group needs to divide into two groups — half playing the roles of the migrants and half the roles of those in the 'host community'.)

2 *Small-group work*
The meeting is asked to break up into smaller groups (about 4) composed of half 'newcomers' and half people who have lived in the community all their lives. Together they are asked to discover how to improve relations between the two groups. They are to list the kinds of action they might take.

3 *Whole-group work*
Each small group reports back and highlights areas of discussion. They read their list of suggestions for improving relations within the community.

4 *Individual work*
Each member of the Inter-racial Club has been given details of the Notting Hill disturbances of 1958. They are asked to speak their 'thoughts aloud' in response to their racialist attacks.

5 *Small-group work*
Contrast the change in relationships within the community by creating *two* group photographs: one to show a typical gathering of people in the black and white community before the summer of 1958 and one to show afterwards.

INFORMING THE DRAMA

Teacher in role as 'community leader' informs the group of the purpose of the meeting. She outlines some of the difficulties the newcomers have had to face in Britain. (See background notes.)

Teacher refers them to background notes and relevant testimony which should help with the discussion.

Someone in the group is asked to record the proposals on the blackboard or on sugar paper.

Teacher can give details of the summer of 1958 in a variety of ways: in role as a 'radio news-announcer', re-reading description in background notes, through discussion of the incidents.

Refer to some of the comments made about the significance of Notting Hill in the background notes.

POINTERS

Clubs such as these were sometimes referred to as Inter-racial Clubs. They were formed in many of the communities in which West Indians came to live.

The objectives of one such club — the Clapham Inter-racial Club — were as follows:

> to promote goodwill between people of all races;
>
> to foster and encourage a spirit of mutual understanding and respect between peoples of all nationalities;
>
> to arrange competitive games, discussions and debates ... and to support activities which will create and maintain good relationships between peoples of all races.

It is important to ensure that the group represents both communities equally. Each small group might want to have a brief question and answer session first to clarify many of their own misunderstandings.

It is important to note that:

> the meetings were friendly and optimistic;
> people rarely spoke about their own discrimination;
> tensions were hidden.

The 'thoughts aloud' can be compiled into a group statement. Copies can be made and distributed to each member of the group.

According to Donald Hinds (1966)
'The Club is mild tempered compared to civil rights organizations. In fact, the Club doesn't encourage debates on race....'

News reports from 2 September, 1958
'Racial tension erupted into daylight yesterday in the Notting Hill area of North Kensington as violence against black people and property broke out.'

'On Bramley Road one house was set alight and two others pelted with bricks and milk bottles. Another house had a bicycle thrown through the window.'

According to a 'Times' report
'A crowd of youths went through Oxford Gardens ... smashing windows in houses where coloured people live. "They didn't miss a house," said one white resident.'

For example, shopping in the market, sitting on the bus, fetching a child from a childminder's — these are all typical meeting-points for both sections of the community.

From Edward Scobie — Black Britannia
'One could not help but notice the fear and suspicion which showed in the faces of black people as they went about their daily business.'

Lesson 9 Bringing up Children

DRAMATIC STRUCTURE	INFORMING THE DRAMA
1 *In pairs* — as parent and daughter/son who is about to leave home for the first time. Parent gives child advice about how best to cope in the new environment.	Each pair may decide on their own situation. For example, whether the young person is going to a new town, college, job, a distant city, etc.
2 *Whole-group work—discussion* Compare the different kinds of advice given by parents.	On large pieces of paper, write down all the different words of advice and display these around the room.
3 *Small-group work* Plan and act out a situation in which the young person in the new environment comes into conflict with one of the values or beliefs held by the parents.	Refer to the 'words of advice' displayed around the room as an aid to working out the situation.
4 *Small-group work* Some consequence occurs as a result of the young person's experience in the new environment. Decide what this consequence is and act out the parents' reaction when they find out about it.	The pupils, drawing on their own experience, will need to discuss: 1 the possible consequences of the young person's conflict; 2 the various perspectives that people of different generations might adopt to these consequences.

POINTERS

In giving this advice the parent will, either intentionally or unintentionally, be expressing some of her basic attitudes towards life.

The display of 'words of advice' can be used as a constant reminder of some of the parent's values and beliefs.

The group can highlight the conflict faced by the younger generation by introducing the parent's viewpoint in the form of a 'voice of conscience': e.g. one of the pupils, speaking as the parent, can repeat some of the advice given by the older generation at significant points in the scene.

After the presentation of each scene, the whole group may wish to interview parent and child together in order to contrast the two views of the situation.

The women involved in *Motherland* gave advice to their daughters about the following:

Education
'Get the best education you can.'

Religion
'If you have that as a young person, you'll have protection for the rest of your life.'

Prejudice
'You have to be careful how you move amongst people.'

Background
'Feel proud of being black.'
'Within a West Indian household you are always in the West Indies.'

The pupils involved in the Project identified some of the following as areas of disagreement with the parent's generation:

Religion	Work
Authority	Leisure
Music	Sex roles
Sex	Food
Education	Teachers
Politics	Nationality
Discipline	Racism
Police	Social welfare
Unemployment	Relationships with people of other races

Lesson 10 On Women

DRAMATIC STRUCTURE

1 *Whole-group work — discussion*
As a class discuss the kinds of pressures that were placed upon women as they began to settle in Britain. Make a list of all the things one woman might have had to concern herself with as she planned for herself and her family on a particular working day.

2 *Individual work—'thoughts aloud'*
Each pupil is asked to take on the role of one of the women who sits down to rest at the end of the day. This is the first time she has stopped to rest, to think, to reflect upon her situation. Each pupil is to speak out a word or a sentence to express the woman's inner thoughts.

3 *Small-group work*
In small groups create a still photograph which represents what, for your group, sums up the experience of one woman.

4 *Small-group work*
Now develop this photograph into a more extended piece of work — a mime, a choral poem, a dance, a song — to create a lasting image of one woman's struggle in Britain.

INFORMING THE DRAMA

Refer back to Part One, sections 4, 5, 6, 7 and 9 which include information about the responsibilities that were placed upon women in the home and at work, in relationships with men and with their children.

Teacher as narrator retells some of the situations faced by one woman on a particular day. The teacher may use this narrative to introduce the 'thoughts aloud'. As each pupil speaks her words, the teacher writes them down and reports them back to the group.

Use a word or words from the 'thoughts aloud' to help 'the audience' understand your photograph.

The group can use any of the words from the 'thoughts aloud' or any of the women's testimony to help them create this final piece of work.

POINTERS

It is important to emphasize that all this has happened to *one woman*. Many of these responsibilities are taken on by the same woman every day.

'A woman will sit down and she knows she will be getting so much money in her hand each week. So much has to be put by, so much has to be sent back to the West Indies. Children have to be brought up, things have to be done and life is just one big planning.'

The pupils may want to close their eyes and the teacher may want to darken the room. The words spoken represent the inner thoughts of the woman. (If some groups find this exercise embarrassing, they can write the thoughts down instead of speaking them out in role and later share them with the rest of the group.)

An example of narration that can be used to introduce 'thoughts aloud':

'It is the end of the day. It is the first chance you have had to sit down, to put your feet up, to relax. The children have been fed, bathed, changed and put to bed. There is silence for the first time in hours and hours. It is 10 o'clock in the evening. You were up at 5 in the morning — finished the washing, did some ironing, got the children up, washed and dressed, caught the bus at 6.30 am to take the children to the minder's — then on to work, worrying about the children at work, working hard all day at the factory, then back to the minder's. Shopping, dinner, household chores, children's needs and now, at the end of the day . . .'

Not all the pupils in the group need to be in the photograph but they all must be involved in creating its effect.

Look at Scene 11 in *Motherland* (The dream sequence) to see one group's response to this task.

SUGGESTED READING

1 Caribbean History
AUGIER, F.R. and GORDON, S.C. (1962) *Sources of West Indian History* London: Longman
*BRATHWAITE, E. (series editor) *The People Who Came* London: Longman Book 1 (1968) NORMAN, A.; Book 2 (1970) PATTERSON, P. and CARNEGIE, J.; Book 3 (1972) BRAITHWAITE, E. and PHILLIPS, A.
*INSTITUTE OF RACE RELATIONS (1982) Book 1 *Roots of Racism*; Book 2 *Patterns of Race Relations* London: Institute of Race Relations
JAMES, C.L.R. (1980) *The Black Jacobins* London: Alison & Busby
LEWIS, A. (1977) *Labour in the West Indies* London: New Beacon Books
WILLIAMS, E. (1983) *From Columbus to Castro: The History of the Caribbean 1492–1969* London: Andre Deutsch

2 History of Black People in Britain
ALEXANDER, Z. and DEWJEE, A. (1981) *Roots in Britain* (pamphlet and exhibition) London: Brent Library Service
ALEXANDER, Z. and DEWJEE, A. (eds) (1984) *Wonderful Adventures of Mrs Seacole in Many Lands* Bristol: Falling Wall Press
*FILE, N. and POWER, C. (1981) *Black Settlers in Britain, 1555–1958* London: Heinemann Educational Books
FRYER, P. (1984) *Staying Power: The History of Black People in Britain* London: Pluto Press
HIRO, D. (1971) *Black British White British* London: Eyre & Spottiswoode
SCOBIE, E. (1972) *Black Britannia: A History of Blacks in Britain* Chicago: Johnson
SHYLLON, F.O. (1974) *Black Slaves in Britain* London: Oxford University Press for Institute of Race Relations
SHYLLON, F.O. (1977) *Black People in Britain, 1555–1833* London: Oxford University Press for Institute of Race Relations

3 West Indian Migration to Britain
DAVISON, R.B. (1962) *West Indian Migrants* London: Oxford University Press for Institute of Race Relations
†EGGINTON, J. (1957) *They Seek a Living* London: Hutchinson
FONER, N. (1979) *Jamaica Farewell: Jamaican Migrants in London* London: Routledge & Kegan Paul
GLASS, R. (1960) *Newcomers* London: Centre for Urban Studies and Allen & Unwin
HINDS, D. (1966) *Journey to an Illusion* London: Heinemann
JONES, C. (1964) 'The Caribbean community in Britain' First published in *Freedomways* vol. 4, no. 3, reprinted in *The Black Liberator* no. 1, December (1978), p. 29–37
†PATTERSON, S. (1965) *Dark Strangers* Harmondsworth: Penguin
PEACH, C. (1963) *West Indian Migration to Britain: A Social Geography* London: Oxford University Press for Institute of Race Relations
†RUCK, S.K. (ed.) (1960) *The West Indian Comes to England* London: Routledge & Kegan Paul
THOMAS-HOPE, E. (1980) Hopes and reality in the West Indian migration to Britain *Oral History* vol. 8, no. 1, Sociology Dept., University of Essex, Colchester

4 Other Studies of Migration
GUYOT, J. et al. (1978) *Migrant Women Speak* London: Search Press

*NATIONAL EXTENSION COLLEGE (1980) *Concord Comics: Cartoon Stories about Immigration* Cambridge: National Extension College

PHIZACKLEA, A. (ed.) (1983) *One Way Ticket: Migration and Female Labour* London: Routledge & Kegan Paul

SELLERS, M.S. (ed.) (1981) *Immigrant Women* Philadelphia: Temple University Press

TIERNEY, J. (1982) 'Race, colonialism and migration' in Tierney, J. (ed.) *Race, Migration and Schooling* London: Holt, Rinehart & Winston

WILSON, A. (1978) *Finding a Voice: Asian Women in Britain* London: Virago

5 Black Women's Studies

AMOS, V. and PARMAR, P. (1981) 'Resistances and Responses: the experiences of black girls in Britain', in McRobbie, A. and McCabe T. (eds.) *Feminism for Girls* London: Routledge & Kegan Paul

CARBY, H. (1982) 'White woman listen: Black feminism and the boundaries of sisterhood' in Centre for Cultural Studies *Empire Strikes Back* London: Hutchinson

DAVIS, A. (1981) *Women, Race and Class* London: The Women's Press

HOOKS, B. (1981) *Ain't I a Woman: Black Women and Feminism* London: Pluto

HULL, G.T., SCOTT, P.B. and SMITH, B. (eds) (1982) *But Some of Us Are Brave: Black Women's Studies* New York: The Feminist Press

LERNER, G. (ed.) (1973) *Black Women in White America* New York: Vintage Books

PRESCOD-ROBERTS, M. and STEELE, N. (1980) *Black Women: Bringing it all Back Home* Bristol: Falling Wall Press

RACE TODAY WOMEN (1974) Black women and nursing: a job like any other *Race Today* vol. 6, no. 8, August

RACE TODAY WOMEN (1975) Caribbean women and the black community *Race Today* vol. 7, no. 5, May

STEADY, F.C. (ed.) (1981) *The Black Woman Cross-Culturally* Cambridge, Mass.: Schenkman

6 Poetry and Fiction

AMBIT 91 (1982) *Caribbean Special Issue* 17 Priory Gardens, London N6

BENNETT, L. (1982) 'Colonization in reverse' in *Selected Poems* Kingston: Sangster Book Stores

BRATHWAITE, E. (1973) *The Arrivants* Oxford: Oxford University Press

EMECHETA, B. (1977) *Second Class Citizen* London: Fontana

LAMMING, G. (1980) *The Emigrants* London: Alison & Busby

MARSHALL, P. (1982) *Brown Girl, Brownstones* London: Virago

NAIPAUL, V.S. (1969) *The Middle Passage* Harmondsworth: Penguin

NICHOLS, G. (1983) *I is a Long Memoried Woman* London: Caribbean Cultural International

SALKEY, A. (ed.) (1960) *West Indian Stories* London: Faber & Faber

SELVON, S. (1956) *The Lonely Londoners* London: Longman

*   particularly for younger readers
†   These books were written in the 1950s and 1960s and are subject to the biases and distortions of their time. Approached critically, however, they can be a useful source of information.

BIBLIOGRAPHY

ALEXANDER, Z. and DEWJEE, A. (1981) *Roots in Britain* (pamphlet and exhibition) London: Brent Library Service

ALEXANDER Z. and DEWJEE, A. (ed.) (1984) *Wonderful Adventures of Mrs Seacole in Many Lands* Bristol: Falling Wall Press

AMBIT 91 (1982) *Caribbean Special Issue* 17 Priory Gardens, London N6

AMOS, V. and PARMAR, P. (1981) 'Resistances and Responses: the experiences of black girls in Britain', in McRobbie, A. and McCabe T. (eds.) *Femisism for Girls* London: Routledge & Kegan Paul

AUGIER, F.R. and GORDON, S.C. (1962) *Sources of West Indian History* London: Longman

BEDDOE, D. (1983) *Discovering Women's History* London: Pandora Press

BELL, R.P., PARKER, B.J., and GUY SHEFTALL, B. (eds) (1979) *Sturdy Black Bridges: Visions of Black Women in Literature* New York: Anchor Books

BENNETT, L. (1982) *Selected Poems* Kingston: Sangster Book Stores

BHAVNANI, K.K. (1982) Racist acts *Spare Rib Magazine* nos. 115, 116, 117

BLOOM, V. (1983) *Touch Mi Tell Mi* London: Bogle-L'Ouverture Pub.

BOWLBY, J. (1953) *Childcare and the Growth of Love* Harmondsworth: Penguin

BOURNE, J. (1983) Towards an anti-racist feminism *Race and Class* vol. xxv, no. 1, summer, Institute of Race Relations

BRATHWAITE, E. (1973) *The Arrivants* Oxford: Oxford University Press

BRATHWAITE, E. (1981) *Folkculture of the Slaves in Jamaica* London: New Beacon Books

BRATHWAITE, E. (series ed.) *The People Who Came* London: Longman Book 1 (1968) NORMAN, A.; Book 2 (1970) PATTERSON, P. and CARNEGIE, J.; Book 3 (1972) BRATHWAITE, E. and PHILLIPS, A.

BROOKS, D. (1975) *Race and Labour in London Transport* London: Oxford University Press for Institute of Race Relations

BLACK SCHOLAR (1979) *Black sexism debate* vol. 10, nos. 8, 9, May–June, P.O. Box 908, Sausalito, California

BLACK SCHOLAR (1981) *The black woman* vol. 12, no. 6, Nov.–Dec., P.O. Box 908, Sausalito, California

CARBY, H. (1982) 'White woman listen: black feminism and the boundaries of sisterhood' in Centre for Contemporary Cultural Studies, *Empire Strikes Back* London: Hutchinson

CENTRE FOR CONTEMPORARY CULTURAL STUDIES (1982) *Empire Strikes Back* London: Hutchinson

CLARKE, E. (1957) *My Mother Who Fathered Me* London: Allen & Unwin

COARD, B. (1971) *How the West Indian Child is Made Educationally Subnormal by the British School System* London: New Beacon Books

COTTLE, T.J. (1978) *Black Testimony* London: Wildwood House

COUNTER INFORMATION SERVICES (1978) 'Racism — Who profits?' London

DAVIDSON, C. and BRONER, E.M. (ed.) (1980) *The Lost Tradition: Mothers and Daughters in Literature* New York: Frederick Ungar

DAVIS, A. (1981) *Women, Race and Class* London: The Women's Press

DAVISON, R.B. (1962) *West Indian Migrants* London: Oxford University Press for Institute of Race Relations

DAVISON, R.B. (1966) *Black British: Immigrants to England* London: Oxford University Press for Institute of Race Relations

DES (1981) *West Indian Children in Our Schools* (Rampton Report) (Interim Report of the Committee of Inquiry into the Education of Children from Ethnic Minority Groups) London: HMSO

DODGSON, E. (1984) 'Drama for a multicultural society' in Hussey, M. and Straker-Welds, M. (eds) *Education for Multicultural Society* London: Bell & Hyman
DODGSON, E. (1982) 'Exploring social issues' in Nixon, J. (ed.) *Drama and the Whole Curriculum* London: Hutchinson
DODGSON, E. (1982) The making of *Motherland, London Drama Magazine* vol. 6, no. 7, winter, 1982: reprinted in *ILEA Multiethnic Education Review* vol. 2, no. 2, summer, 1983
DODGSON, E. (1982) 'Working in a south London school' in Wootton, M. (ed.) *New Directions in Drama Teaching* London: Heinemann
EDWARDS, V.K. (1979) *The West Indian Language Issue in British Schools* London: Routledge & Kegan Paul
EGGINTON, J. (1957) *They Seek a Living* London: Hutchinson
EMECHETA, B. (1977) *Second Class Citizen* London: Fontana
FIGUEROA, J. (1982) *An Anthology of African and Caribbean Writing in English* London: Heinemann Educational Books in association with the Open University
FILE, N. and POWER, C. (ed.) (1981) *Black Settlers in Britain 1555—1958* London: Heinemann Educational Books
FONER, N. (1979) *Jamaica Farewell: Jamaican Migrants in London* London: Routledge & Kegan Paul
FRYER, P. (1984) *Staying Power: The History of Black People in Britain* London: Pluto Press
FULLER, M. (1982) 'Young, Female and Black' in Cashmore, E. and Troyna B. (eds.) *Black Youth in Crisis* London: Allen & Unwin
GLASS, R. (1960) *Newcomers* London: Centre for Urban Studies and Allen & Unwin
GUYOT, J. et al. (1979) *Migrant Women Speak* London: Search Press
HINDS, D. (1966) *Journey to an Illusion* London: Heinemann
HIRO, D. (1971) *Black British White British* London: Eyre & Spottiswoode
HOOKS, B.(1982) *Ain't I a Woman: Black Women and Feminism* London: Pluto
HULL, G.T., SCOTT, P.B. and SMITH, B. (1982) *But Some of Us Are Brave: Black Women's Studies* New York: The Feminist Press
INSTITUTE OF RACE RELATIONS (1982) Book 1 *Roots of Racism;* Book 2 *Patterns of Racism* Institute of Race Relations, 247/49 Pentonville Road, London N1
JACKSON, B. & J. (1981) *Childminder* Harmondsworth: Penguin Books
JAMES, C.L.R. (1980) *The Black Jacobins* London: Allison & Busby
JAMES, C.L.R. (1984) *At the Rendezvous of Victory* London: Allison & Busby
JONES, C. (1964) 'The Caribbean community in Britain' first published in *Freedomways* vol. 4, no. 3, reprinted in *The Black Liberator* no. 1, December 1978, pp. 29—37
JUSTUS, J.B. (1981) 'Women's role in West Indian society' in Steady, F.C. (ed.) *The Black Woman Cross-Culturally* Cambridge, Mass.: Schenkman Pub. Co.
LAMMING, G. (1960) *The Pleasures of Exile* London: Michael Joseph
LAMMING, G. (1980) *The Emigrants* London: Allison & Busby
LAWRENCE, E. (1982) 'Just plain commonsense: the roots of racism' in Centre for Contemporary Cultural Studies *Empire Strikes Back* London: Hutchinson
LERNER, G. (ed.) (1973) *Black Women in White America: A Documentary History* New York: Vintage Books
LEWIS, A. (1978) *Labour in the West Indies* London: New Beacon Books
MARSHALL, P. (1982) *Brown Girl, Brownstones* London: Virago
MILES, R. (1982) *Racism and Migrant Labour* London: Routledge & Kegan Paul
MORDECAI, P. and MORRIS, M. (ed.) (1980) *Jamaica Woman: An Anthology of Poems* Kingston: Heinemann Educational Books
NAIPAUL, V.S. (1969) *The Middle Passage* Harmondsworth: Penguin
NATIONAL EXTENSION COLLEGE (1980) *Concord Comics: Cartoon Stories about Immigration* 18 Brooklands Avenue, Cambridge
NICHOLS, G. (1983) *I is a Long Memoried Woman* London: Caribbean Cultural International
NIXON, J. (ed.) (1982) *Drama and the Whole Curriculum* London: Hutchinson
NIXON, J. (1982) 'Case studies' in Stenhouse, L. et al. *Teaching about Race Relations: Problems and Effects* London: Routledge & Kegan Paul

O'NEILL, C. and LAMBERT, A. (1982) *Drama Structures* London: Hutchinson
OPEN UNIVERSITY (1982) *Migration and Settlement in Britain* Block 1, Unit 2, Milton Keynes, Open University Press
PARMAR, P. (1982) 'Gender race and class: Asian women in resistance' in Centre for Contemporary Cultural Studies *Empire Strikes Back* London: Hutchinson
PATTERSON, S. (1965) *Dark Strangers* Harmondsworth: Penguin
PEACH, C. (1968) *West Indian Migration to Britain: A Social Geography* London: Oxford University Press for Institute of Race Relations
PHILLIPS, A.S. (1973) *Adolescence in Jamaica* Kingston: Macmillan
PHIZACKLEA, A. (ed.) (1983) *One Way Ticket: Migration and Female Labour* London: Routledge & Kegan Paul
PRESCOD-ROBERTS, M. and STEELE, N. (1980) *Black Women: Bringing it All Back Home* Bristol: Falling Wall Press
RACE TODAY WOMEN (1974) Black women and nursing: a job like any other *Race Today* vol. 6, no. 8, August
RACE TODAY WOMEN (1975) Caribbean women and the black community *Race Today* vol. 7, no. 5, May
ROSE, E.J.B. et al. (1969) *Colour and Citizenship: A Report on British Race Relations* London: Oxford University Press for Institute of Race Relations
ROWBOTHAM, S. (1973) *Hidden from History* London: Pluto
RUCK, S.K. (ed.) (1960) *The West Indian Comes to England* London: Routledge & Kegan Paul
RUNNYMEDE TRUST AND RADICAL STATISTICS RACE GROUP (1980) *Britain's Black Population* London: Heinemann Educational Books
RUTTER, M. (1972) *Maternal Deprivation Reassessed* Harmondsworth: Penguin
SALKEY, A. (ed.) (1960) *West Indian Stories* London: Faber & Faber
SALKEY, A. (1980) *Away* London: Allison & Busby
SCOBIE, E. (1972) *Black Britannia: A History of Blacks in Britain* Chicago: Johnson
SELLER, M.S. (ed.) (1981) *Immigrant Women* Philadelphia: Temple University Press
SELVON, S. (1956) *The Lonely Londoners* London: Longman
SHARPE, S. (1976) *Just Like a Girl: How Girls Learn to be Women* Harmondsworth: Penguin
SHYLLON, F.O. (1974) *Black Slaves in Britain* London: Oxford University Press for Institute of Race Relations
SHYLLON, F.O. (1977) *Black People in Britain 1555—1833* London: Oxford University Press for Institute of Race Relations
SIVANANDAN, A. (1982) *A Different Hunger: Writings on Black Resistance* London: Pluto
SMITH, B. (ed.) (1983) *Home Girls: A Black Feminist Anthology* New York: Kitchen Table, Woman of Color Press
SMITH, D. (1977) *Racial Disadvantage in Britain* Harmondsworth: Penguin
STEADY, F.C. (ed.) (1981) *The Black Woman Cross-Culturally* Cambridge, Mass.: Schenkman
STONE, M. (1981) *The Education of the Black Child in Britain: The Myth of Multiracial Education* London: Fontana
THOMAS-HOPE, E. (1980) Hopes and reality in the West Indian migration to Britain *Oral History* vol. 8, no. 1, Sociology Dept., University of Essex, Colchester
TIERNEY, J. (1982) 'Race, colonialism and migration' in Tierney, J. (ed.) *Race, Migration and Schooling* London: Holt, Rinehart & Winston
TIERNEY, J. (ed.) (1982) *Race, Migration and Schooling* London: Holt, Rinehart & Winston
WALKER, A. (1975) *Goodnight Willie Lee, I'll See You in the Morning* New York: The Dial Press
WALVIN, J. (1971) *The Black Presence: A Documentary History of the Negro in England* London: Orbach & Chambers
WILLIAMS, E. (1964) *Capitalism and Slavery* London: Deutsch
WILLIAMS, E. (1983) *From Columbus to Castro — The History of the Caribbean 1492—1969* London: Deutsch
WILSON, A. (1978) *Finding a Voice: Asian Women in Britain* London: Virago